# ADVANCE PRAISE

"*A Great Move* is everything you need to make a successful expatiate assignment. With all the bases covered, Katia superbly captures the fundamental thoughts, emotions and drivers crucial in deciding to leave the comfort of your home (or country), enjoying the assignment adventure, all while achieving your personal and professional goals."

**Paul Kelly**, Global Relocation & Immigration
Program Manager, Intel Corporation

"Finally, a book about moving abroad that addresses the social, emotional and psychological, along with the physical, practical and career considerations! *A Great Move* covers all the bases, outlining the five areas that truly matter and demand your attention as you move through the stages of deciding, preparing, moving and settling in a different country or culture. The balance between information, empathy and guidance is perfect, with stories of actual expat experiences woven throughout, along with snapshot assessments, chapter Checklists, and Common Mistakes. This book will help you create the conditions for having the challenging, yet compulsory caring conversations, connection and clarity needed when considering an international move, and the tools to help make the ensuing transitions shorter, softer and steadier."

**Linda Janssen,** author of *The Emotionally Resilient Expat:
Engage, Adapt and Thrive Across Cultures*

Published by
**LID Publishing Limited**
The Record Hall, Studio 204,
16-16a Baldwins Gardens,
London EC1N 7RJ, UK

524 Broadway, 11th Floor, Suite 08-120,
New York, NY 10012, US

info@lidpublishing.com
www.lidpublishing.com

A member of:

www.businesspublishersroundtable.com

Printed in Great Britain by TJ International
ISBN: 978-1-911498-60-5

Cover design: Caroline Li
Layout: Matthew Renaudin

# A

**KATIA VLACHOS**

# GREAT

# MOVE

## SURVIVING AND THRIVING IN YOUR EXPAT ASSIGNMENT

LONDON        NEW YORK        SHANGHAI
MADRID         BARCELONA       BOGOTA
MEXICO CITY    MONTERREY       BUENOS AIRES

# CONTENTS

## INTRODUCTION 2

Why it's important to make a great move. Why expat assignments fail. The importance of paying attention to family concerns. Moving as a multi-phase process of deciding, preparing, moving and settling in.

## PART I: INTENTION AND THE RIGHT PRINCIPLES 10

Why you should think hard about your intention for the move. Avoiding rushing headlong into making a move. Thinking through what would make the move a great one. Understanding the five core principles to guide your move.

### 1. PRINCIPLE #1: YOUR CONCEPT OF HOME MATTERS 16

Why it's important to understand your concept of home, and that of others you'll be moving with. How to assess the extent to which your concept of home is about place, people and feeling. Why your concept of home should shape every phase of the moving process.

### 2. PRINCIPLE #2: THE PROCESS OF TRANSITION MATTERS 30

Understanding the stages of psychological adjustment that happen during a move. Anticipating how you and other family members will experience the adjustment process. Recognizing when you and others are moving between stages.

### 3. PRINCIPLE #3: YOU MATTER 39

Understanding how your personality will influence your adjustment process. Gaining deeper insight into your personality and its impact on how you move. Assessing and building your flexibility and resilience.

## 8. MOVING 146

Making a good departure by anticipating the best ways to say goodbye and to stay in touch. Getting the help you need during the move. Collecting or creating keepsakes. Being strategic about the packing and unpacking process. Taking care of yourself and your family during the moving process.

## 9. SETTLING IN 160

Planning to create home in your new residence as soon as possible. Helping your children create a sense of home in their rooms. Retaining important family rituals. Beginning the process of engaging with the new location and culture. Building your support network. Having a 'Plan B'.

## 10. MOVING AS A SINGLE EXPAT 188

The special challenges of moving as a single. Looking before leaping when you make the decision. Identifying the full range of potential support your employer can offer. Thinking through the choices and trade-offs when deciding where to live. Enlisting support throughout the move. Taking care of yourself through the process.

## CONCLUSION: YOUR GREAT MOVE 208

Bringing it all together.
Diving into the expat journey.
Preparing to be changed.

# ACKNOWLEDGMENTS

Writing this book has been a journey. This journey has brought me knowledge and insights into what shapes the expat experience; it has allowed me to reflect, make connections, discuss, and test my assumptions – all while making my own expat transitions; it has helped me redefine my concept of home. Most importantly, this journey has taken me into the lives, hearts and minds of dozens of people leading globally mobile lives. I want to acknowledge them first. They are the ones who shared their experiences, concerns, triumphs and struggles with me, sometimes on more than one occasion, with openness, generosity and patience, and for that, I am truly grateful. Their stories have inspired, educated, guided and challenged me. They have accompanied me on this journey.

Thank you to my book coach Caroline Allen of *Art of Storytelling*, who put her heart and soul – in addition to her incredible writing skills and insight – into my book project. And who, instead of rolling her eyes, stuck with me when, almost at the final stages, I decided to start over and re-write the whole book. A writer could not ask for a better 'travel' companion.

Thank you to David Creelman, who kindly took the time to brainstorm with me when I was looking into publishing the book, and to Lukas Michel, who was generous enough to put me in touch with his publisher, who then became my publisher.

Thank you to Martin Liu, of LID Publishing, for taking up *A Great Move* and for putting together the wonderful team who contributed to the publication of this book. Special thanks to my fantastic editor, Sara Taheri, who helped me tighten the manuscript and bring out the essence of my message, and to the tireless Niki Mullin, who promoted the hell out of that message and was always there to answer my (many) questions. Also, I would like to thank Caroline Li, for the beautiful cover design and for being so responsive to all my requests until we got to the final version; Miro Iliev for working with me to create the book's online 'home'; and Charlotte Reynard, for working hard to organize the book launch event.

To Neil Bothams of Santa Fe relocation, thank you for believing in *A Great Move* and for graciously co-hosting its launch and thanks to everyone at Santa Fe who worked on promoting the book.

To my global nomad friends, spread out around the world: you are the reason I wrote this book. I can't thank you enough for your generosity, whether it was offering (naively, unsuspectingly) to be my 'guinea pigs' by taking part in my first, exploratory interviews; discussing my ideas and vetting my outlines along the way; patiently answering my questions when I kept coming back for follow-up interviews; or cheering me on every step of the way. This book would not have been possible without your kindness and support. You are my family and I owe you gratitude for teaching me that home is where your tribe is.

To my husband, Michael, thank you for being with me on this journey, from convincing me that the ideas sketched out on a paper napkin in a Viennese café were the perfect outline for a book, to editing my manuscript before I sent it out for publication. Having you by my side as my advocate, advisor and biggest fan (even if I will always believe you're biased) has made all the difference.

Last, but not least, to my three beautiful Third Culture Kids, thank you for being such wonderful moving partners – even when you did not really have a choice – and for teaching me how to do things right, or rather how not to mess things up, when moving with children. For tolerating my constant busy-ness, even when you did not fully understand what my book is about. And for wanting "to write books like Mama" when you grow up. I owe you eternal gratitude, for being my inspiration, my source of strength, and my home.

For everyone reading this book, I will leave you with the final lines Calvin says to Hobbes in Bill Watterson's last cartoon strip, published on 31 December, 1995:

*"It's a magical world, Hobbes, ol' buddy... Let's go exploring!"*

# FOREWORD

Making big decisions is never easy; there is always risk.

In my experience, as my career developed and my family grew, the factors affecting my decisions became increasingly complex. Making personal decisions generally requires an intimate and honest understanding of self. What drives me? What are my values? How do I interact best with others? You look to yourself for answers.

Trying to make decisions for other people, however, is harder still. As you navigate decisions for your partner, your children or your team, the factors you must manage become more convoluted and difficult to balance. You try your best to find the perfect solution, but it is impossible to get everything right. You might think that managing your expectations and being realistic is common sense, especially when planning something as life-changing as an international move. However, the emotional weight of our decisions can be deceptive. We often neglect to think about the emotional impact of change – on ourselves and those around us – because decision-making seems so strategic.

Careful planning, organization and expert execution are viewed as the traditional keys to success in business. However, as we will explore, it is important to anticipate how you and those around you will react to such change *emotionally*. Change is not finite; it is a process of discovering, disassembling and reassembling what you want and where you want to be. You must learn to adapt and then adapt again, accepting support where you can.

Since joining a leading global mobility company, I have become immersed in an environment that thrives on supporting individuals and families as they change their lives forever. Thousands of individuals relocate around the world on a regular basis, all of whom have different requirements, resources and priorities.

As any of our experienced experts will tell you, no two relocations are ever the same. Leaving your familiar surroundings and finding a new home, especially when moving abroad, is a hugely personal and daunting adventure. There are so many factors to consider, with so many changing variables, that it is normal to feel overwhelmed. Once you have made the decision to relocate, a million more decisions follow. Usually, by the time you have found a new home, a new routine and rekindled a feeling of stability, you will realize that your eventual outcome is vastly different from your original expectations. This is not a bad thing; the decisions we make never go exactly to plan; adaptability is a necessary human strength.

So, as you read this book, it is important to gather information and seek support. Be kind to yourself and divide your energy thoughtfully between the emotional and strategic aspects of your move. The principles of a healthy move, which this book will outline and guide you through, are about establishing your resources and putting yourself and your loved ones first. The more open and adaptable you are during your decision-making process, the more you enable yourself to work, live and thrive in new places around the world. In my experience, learning to make informed and passionate decisions without fear – both in my personal life and in the workplace – has been invaluable. Although it is rarely possible to make a perfect choice, you can always perfect your decision-making process. Have you noticed that when you see change as an exciting and unpredictable adventure, you discover a greater sense of fulfilment and purpose? My experience has taught me to be adaptable, seek expertise and commit to change. Yes, there will be risk, but this will never be without reward.

**Neil Bothams**
CEO Europe, Santa Fe Relocation
www.santaferelo.com

To my father, who showed me how
to find home in the world.

# INTRODUCTION

When Tom was offered a position at his investment bank's subsidiary in Frankfurt, Germany, Amanda agreed that the timing was perfect. While they were born and had lived in the US – Tom in Colorado, Amanda in southern California – they had travelled extensively internationally. Their children, a four-year-old boy and a five-month-old girl, were young and portable.

For Amanda, Tom's job offer had come at a time when she was already at a career crossroad. She had just returned to work after a short maternity leave. Even with childcare, she was finding it hard to keep up with the pace of her work as a corporate lawyer. She longed for some time off to spend with her children, and an expat assignment seemed like an ideal opportunity. It provided a good rationale for taking a career break and focusing on her family and even finally having some time for herself.

Pressed to make a quick decision, Tom accepted the position and Amanda quit her job. He had to leave for Frankfurt almost immediately, while she stayed behind with the children to manage the logistics of the move. That was quite a challenge, given that she still had to work through her notice period and was, for now, living like a single parent. Tom's employer put them in touch with a relocation service provider, which offered basic services, including a moving company specializing in overseas relocation and a local housing agent in Frankfurt.

Amanda and the kids moved to Europe four months later. The time apart from Tom had been tough, and Amanda was excited and relieved when the family was, at last, reunited. Fortunately, the housing agent helped them secure a beautiful apartment in a residential suburb in the outskirts of town, and they moved in. While neither Tom nor Amanda spoke German, they had decided that full immersion was the best (and only) way for their children to learn the language, so their son immediately joined the local kindergarten (for ages 3 to 6). Amanda had started online German lessons a few weeks before the move, but was nowhere near conversational.

Tom's new position required him to work long hours and travel two to three days a week. Feeling isolated and somewhat abandoned, Amanda quickly grew frustrated. She loved their apartment, but it was a 40-minute bus ride from the city centre, and a 15-minute walk from the nearest supermarket. Travelling by public transport with a baby in a stroller and a four-year-old in tow was a major operation. Her son's kindergarten ended at noon, so her afternoons alone with the two children were long. She had not thought about organizing childcare, assuming she would not need it since she was not working. With Tom gone most of the time, she was a single parent again. By the time evenings came, she was physically and emotionally exhausted.

Tom, meanwhile, was having a much easier time adjusting. He was working for the same company, everyone spoke English, the business was familiar, and he had colleagues to whom he could turn for support. In contrast to the ready-made support system that work provided him with, Amanda had to create hers (and her family's) from scratch.

Within a couple months, the adjustment challenges started to take a toll on their relationship. The few times that Tom came home early enough for dinner, Amanda was snappy and resentful. To make matters worse, their son became moody, was constantly tired, and regularly threw temper tantrums. Tom attributed it to his son's age and getting used to life with a new younger sibling. Amanda was concerned the issues were deeper and had to deal with the consequences. This created still more stress and tension in their relationship.

Things came to a head when their daughter became sick. Tom was, again, largely absent and Amanda found herself trying to navigate the German healthcare system without the necessary language skills. She became increasingly despondent and started wondering whether she should go back to the US with the kids. Tom felt caught in a vice between the demands of work and the family's distress. On the one hand, he felt the need to live up to the responsibilities of his new position, and on the other, he knew he needed to help manage the situation at home.

Amanda began to pressure Tom to move back to the US. He knew that returning from his international assignment earlier than planned, most likely without a new position back at headquarters, would be a serious career setback. Still, after just a year in Frankfurt, with their relationship frayed, Amanda verging on depression and Tom's career hanging in the balance, they decided to head home.

Tom and Amanda exemplify what *not* to do when making an international move. With forethought and planning, many of the stresses they faced could have been avoided or managed with greater success. Understanding how to make a successful international move is not just about avoiding broken careers and the financial toll; it's also about maintaining mental and physical health, nurturing relationships and preserving satisfying family lives.

If you are contemplating whether to take an international assignment or are likely to do so in the future, this book is for you. It will show you how to anticipate and prepare for the challenges, as well as provide you with a detailed roadmap for making the move a success. If your partner is the one potentially embarking on an expat assignment, this book will help you ensure that your career is not damaged in the process and show you how to feel at home more rapidly in your new location. If you are a parent moving abroad, this book will show you how to help your children make a smooth transition and learn to thrive in their new environment.

If you are a corporate sponsor and want to know how to maximize the chances of making high-risk international assignments succeed, this book will provide you with a framework and tools. Finally, if you work with or support expatriates, it will help you gain insights into how expatriates think and how they approach transitions; how they perceive home and how that affects their coping mechanisms when they move; and what shapes their experience and how you can help them make the most of it.

Tom and Amanda are part of a growing trend towards global mobility. As of the end of 2017, there are expected to be about 57 million expatriates worldwide, which includes individual workers, students, retirees, corporate assignees and their unemployed spouses and children.[1] Research shows that international assignee levels have increased by 25% over the past decade and are expected to rise a further 50% by 2020.[2] According to a Global Mobility Trends Survey in 2016, 75% of respondents – global mobility professionals – expected the growth rate of their international assignments to either increase or stay the same in 2017-18.[3]

International assignments are not only valued by organizations, ambitious professionals often see them as a prerequisite for career advancement and an important part of personal development. According to a survey by PwC,[4] 71% of millennials say they want and expect an international assignment during their career.

International assignments are big investments. It costs an average of $311,000 per year to send an employee abroad.

A typical three-year expat assignment is, on average, a million-dollar investment.[5] The 'expat package', including compensation, allowances (such as moving expenses, training, housing subsidies and cost-of-living adjustments), long-term benefits (employer contributions to pension, healthcare plans, disability and life insurance) and management costs (the costs to the organization of supporting their expatriate programs, such as devoted staff and outsourced services) is estimated to be more than three, and up to seven, times the cost of a local employee.[6]

While estimates vary, between 4 and 10% of expatriate assignments get terminated early.[7] Assignment failure takes a heavy toll – financial, professional and emotional – on those who move, their families and their sponsors. For the expatriate and their family, a failed assignment can cause career setback and significant emotional stress. Personal costs include reduced self-esteem and tensions within the family, resulting in damaged relationships, potential substance abuse and depression. These personal issues can turn into company costs through lower employee performance and productivity, and the unwillingness of colleagues to accept an expatriate assignment themselves. Other indirect organizational costs include damage to the business, costs of replacement, low employee morale and loss of valuable talent. The direct costs to corporate sponsors are estimated to be three to five times the assignee's annual salary.

Why do expat assignments fail? Like Tom and Amanda, many expats make uninformed decisions and move with minimal preparation. They have unrealistic expectations of what an international move entails, both in practical and emotional terms, so they neglect to build up sufficient resources to deal with the consequences. This substantially increases the odds that their moves will fail, which usually means that, like Tom, the assignee will return home before the end of the assignment. 'Family concerns' are the top stated reason for early assignment return. These include the inability of the spouse and/or children to adjust to the new location, spouse/partner career issues, concerns about the children's education, health matters, quality of life and lack of practical support. Almost 70% of expatriate employees move with a partner or spouse.[8] When partners are unhappy with their new homes, it sets up assignments for failure.

The good news is that most failures of expat assignments are avoidable. Many of the challenges expatriates face are predictable and can be mitigated with careful forethought and planning. Adjusting to a new environment and culture, immersing oneself into a new life – both professional and private – and navigating culture shock, all at the same time, are big challenges. However, adopting the *right guiding principles* and using the *right process* to prepare for and make an international move can significantly increase your odds of success.

The first section of this book outlines the right guiding principles, followed by a detailed, systematic approach for the process of moving. An international move is a multi-phase process, starting with decision-making, and followed by preparation, execution of the move, and finally, settling in. Each phase consists of key activities and decisions.

Whether you are moving alone or as part of a family, this book provides you with a systematic, step-by-step guide for deciding, planning and carrying out that move, and offers specific strategies you can use to not only anticipate and overcome challenges, but also to thrive in your global life and find home anywhere in the world. Although written about international moves, the principles, insights and strategies presented here are relevant and applicable to all kinds of moves. These transitions pose similar challenges, whether one moves internationally, within the same country or even within the same city or town.

*A Great Move* draws on in-depth interviews, as well as case studies and anecdotes that cover a range of expatriate experiences, lifestyles and perspectives – from dual-career couples navigating consecutive moves, to 'trailing spouses' following their partners' job-driven itineraries, to diplomatic families and single 'career nomads' leading a globe-trotting life.

Five years after Tom and Amanda moved back to the US, they were settled and thriving. But it took them some time to rebuild their lives. Amanda left her corporate law career track and discovered her passion to be a writer and a blogger. While she is happy with her new career direction, thinking back, she says that she would have liked to have had a clearer picture of her professional options and constraints before moving to Germany. She could have, for example, hired a coach to help her navigate her career transition and make the most of her time there. She also realizes how childcare could have helped enormously during their time abroad.

For several months after they returned home, Tom struggled to find a suitable new position in his firm. Those first months back were taxing professionally and personally. He was always on edge, which also strained his marriage and relationship with his children. Eventually, an attractive opportunity came up, which allowed him to bounce back. In retrospect, he says he should have been more aware of the challenges his family would face and should have made sure that he was available for them in those critical first few months of adjustment. He should have used that knowledge to manage expectations at work and budget the time he would need to support Amanda and the children.

Neither Tom nor Amanda regret the move. However, were they to do it again, they would do many things differently. For example, they would plan for adequate childcare before arriving in the new location, start learning the language earlier, find an apartment in the centre of town, organize age-appropriate support for their children and seek help in navigating the healthcare system.

An international move can be a life-changing journey. It can be stimulating, energizing, enriching and inspiring.

But it can also be challenging, confusing, frustrating and messy, especially during the transition. It is my hope that this book will provide you with solid foundations for making a smooth and successful transition. More than that, I hope that it will help you cope with the challenges, so that you can focus on making the most of your expat experience and building a thriving new global life.

With that, let's dig into setting your intention and adopting the basic principles for making a successful expat move.

# PART I

# INTENTION
# AND THE RIGHT
# PRINCIPLES

In the Buddhist tradition, right intention (or right thought) is the practice of being mindful of how our aspirations shape the way we think and act. When you are launching into something as challenging as making an international move, you should take time to establish your intention: not just what you plan to do or achieve – your purpose – but also your determination, attitude and resolve. What are your goals? What do you want to accomplish? What principles will guide your choices? How do you want to *be* through this experience? These simple yet powerful questions will help you gain the clarity of intention you need to make the right decisions and achieve the right outcomes. The concept also has attracted interest in the field of business,[1] where researchers have examined how leaders construct and communicate intention, and how that motivates employees, shapes performance and predicts successful results.

Whether seen from a spiritual, business or personal perspective, intention allows us to see the big picture. Clarity of intention is especially important when it comes to big decisions and life-changing moments. Being mindful and clear about what we want to achieve makes the difference between just getting through and making the most of a challenging situation, a tough decision or a difficult task.

How does intention apply to making international moves? Many of us, in our thirst for adventure or simply because of lack of time, rush headfirst into a move without reflecting on our goals – what we want out of the experience. Often, we end up being pulled in different directions, muddling (or worse, struggling) through successive challenges, trying to make it through each day without having in mind the big picture or a vision of our desired outcome.

What should be your intention when making a move and how do you go about setting that intention? Ask yourself these questions: What would make this move a great move for you? What do you want to achieve? A thriving professional career? A happy and balanced family life? A satisfied spouse? Well-adjusted children? All of the above? Ask questions that connect you to your goals, your reason for making the move, your ultimate 'why'.

The answers will help keep you on track when times are challenging or when you feel overwhelmed. They will connect you with your intention throughout the phases of the move, *especially* when you are going through tough times. That's why it's important to write your intention down, print it out and have it in front of you, somewhere in your home or office where you will see it every day.

In my years of research and hundreds of conversations with expatriates, I have discovered that there are five key principles that apply to most moves and that can help you in setting and connecting to your intention. These basic rules will guide your thinking and actions through every phase of the move. I call them the *right principles*, and they are the foundation of the systematic approach for making a great move that I present in this book.

## Principle #1: Your Concept of Home Matters

What is home to you? This is important to understand, because your concept of home (and that of others with whom you move) will pervade all dimensions of your life as an expat. Creating home is an essential part of the moving and transition process and a crucial determinant of success. Your concept(s) of home shape the way you make moves and cope with adjustment challenges. The concept of home principle and its implications are explored in Chapter 1.

## Principle #2: The Process of Transition Matters

Becoming familiar with the stages of adaptation to a new location allows you to manage expectations of adjustment, as well as to anticipate and prepare to address potential challenges. Knowing that there is a pattern in the process of adjustment, and that everyone goes through it, will help you deal with the challenges of moving, and help you support your loved ones as they confront their own challenges. The process of transition and its implications for making a great move are discussed in Chapter 2.

### Principle #3: You Matter

Your personal attributes will influence how well and quickly you adjust to new environments. Flexibility, openness, willingness to take risks, resilience and entrepreneurship are just some of the personality traits and skills that make a 'good expat'. Getting a sense of how 'fit' you are for expatriate life, in terms of the traits, abilities and skills you already have, and those that you need to work on, will help you manage your expectations of adjustment. It will also allow you to focus on developing the right skill set to thrive in your new environment. The importance of personality traits and skills is examined in Chapter 3.

### Principle #4: Your Partner Matters

Many expatriates move accompanied by a partner, spouse or other family members (children, parents). While moving as a single person comes with its own set of challenges, moving with a partner tends to increase the level of complexity. How well your partner or spouse fares through a move can make or break it. That's why it's important to take into account their needs, expectations, personality and concepts of home, and provide them with the support they need. The complexities and challenges of moving with a partner, but also the importance of prioritizing the relationship through a move, are discussed in Chapter 4.

### Principle #5: Your Children Matter

Children experience transitions differently than adults do. It is important to understand the particular challenges they may face, depending on factors such as their personality and age, so that you can support them appropriately through the transition. The children's perspective of a move and the challenges they are likely to face are discussed in more detail in Chapter 5.

The next five chapters will help you understand these principles so that you can apply them to make a great move. Most of the chapters include diagnostic tools for assessing your own situation. At the end of each chapter, I include a checklist for applying each principle.

# 1

**PRINCIPLE #1:**
YOUR CONCEPT OF
HOME MATTERS

*"… homesickness meant different things to
different people at different times.
Some who used the word, longed for family,
some for houses, others for towns and landscapes,
for all of these were constituents of the idea of home."*

**Susan J. Matt,** *Homesickness: An American History*

On a clear August morning in Zurich, Switzerland, I drive
my two older children to their first day at a new school. We
have just moved to Zurich from Vienna, Austria. Along the
coast of Lake Zurich, I take in the magnificent scenery – the
water on one side, the vineyards on the other, the mountains
in the background. We arrived here a week earlier; I hardly
know the city, but feel a powerful, visceral connection to the
landscape. I think to myself, *I could really feel at home here.*

I grew up in Athens, but Zurich still hits me with a feeling
of home. Raised on the Mediterranean, living in a city on the
water – even if it's not salt water, even if the actual city looks
nothing like my hometown – is evocative. It is a formidable,
instinctive recognition, one I have felt before in other places
where I lived close to water. I promise myself that, if I can
help it, from now on, I will only move to places that evoke
these feelings.

Why do we feel at home in some places but not in others?
Why is the connection so powerful sometimes, while other
times we struggle to find one at all? This has a lot to do with
our concept of home: how we perceive home and how that
perception shapes the way we create home when we move.

Home is a universal human need. But for expats and
global nomads, who take the leap outside the conventional
paradigm of home, it is even more crucial. Your concept of

home is a key ingredient of your mobile life – it shapes how you experience that life. To understand how your concept of home guides the way you move, let's first explore a few different concepts.

I grew up with a conventional definition of home. I spent most of my childhood in the same house, same neighbourhood and same city. I went to the same school from grade one through to high school graduation. I spent every summer at the same seaside resort with the same families. I had the same group of friends throughout my childhood. Their presence, and that of my family, was a constant, something I could count on. I recall few goodbyes and a lot of stability, continuity and predictability.

At 24, I left my hometown to pursue a graduate degree in Boston. Standing at the departure gate at Athens airport, I knew I would not be coming back. I wanted to explore the world. My journey ultimately would take me from Boston to Paris to Los Angeles to Vienna to Zurich, and it did not occur to me that my sense of home would be transformed in the process.

While I was gone, my home country changed. I was too far away to keep up with new developments, events and cultural references. The people I loved changed and I was not always around to share their lives, milestones, triumphs and disappointments. I changed, as well. Every new place, every new experience shaped me and made me into a person very different from the one I would have been had I stayed in Athens. 'Home' and I did not fit together anymore. Beyond the automatic answer – "I am from Greece" – I was no longer sure where home was.

I began to look for home elsewhere. Choosing to lead an expat lifestyle, essentially to be a permanent foreigner, meant that I valued my mobility so much that I was willing to give up attachment to a specific place, even if I was not fully conscious of the implications of that choice.

Home took on different dimensions. In Los Angeles, home was the feeling of freedom, creativity, vitality and unlimited possibilities. In Vienna, home was people, the relationships I built and cherished, with friends who became my extended family. In Zurich, home has a physical dimension, that of comfort and peace in a landscape that speaks to my soul and makes me feel rooted. I create home again and again with each move.

There are probably as many definitions of home as there are people. As part of my research for this book, I interviewed men and women of different ages, backgrounds and stories. I discussed home with a man who changed houses, friends and schools almost every year in his early childhood; a multicultural, dual-career married couple in a long-distance relationship; a musician who felt that he belonged equally to three different homes in three different countries; and a single expat who fell in love with and found home in a country she had known nothing about when she first visited. Despite their different life stories, these people are united by their mobile lifestyle. All have moved at least once – most, several times – as children, as adults or both.

Our conversations focused on questions such as: What is home for you? What do you need to feel at home? How do you go about creating home? These questions were not new to them. Some had a hard time defining home, while others could not settle on a single definition. Some felt at home everywhere, and some didn't think they could settle anywhere. The perceptions of home covered a spectrum from the literal to the abstract, the physical to the emotional. Gradually, as I did more interviews, however, three concepts of home emerged: Home as a Place, Home as a Feeling and Home as People.

## HOME AS A PLACE

This is the traditional definition of home, where geography is the defining aspect. The geography of home is not one-dimensional. Home can be our passport country; the city, town or village where we grew up; the neighbourhood where we spent formative years and made lifelong friends; the house or apartment that features in our childhood memories. Home can be a specific room, such as our childhood bedroom, the attic where we played hide-and-seek, the dining room that hosted our family dinners. Home can also be a landscape that speaks to our soul. There are places that make us feel rooted and connected in a visceral way, either because they hold powerful memories or because they remind us of places that do.

This traditional definition of home is becoming less and less relevant for global nomads. The more we move, and the earlier in life, the less important any particular place becomes. The globally mobile don't always have the connection and continuity from childhood to adulthood or roots that go back generations. However, place still plays a powerful role in their lives. As Indian psychoanalyst and cultural writer Sudhir Kakar, said: "… the longing for place can be buried or denied or suppressed in the placeless, but it will never truly go away."[1] We long for place, even if we cannot always agree on just one place.

## HOME AS A FEELING

Home, whether it is linked to a particular place or not, is an emotional concept, a feeling, a state of mind. In his 1985 essay, "The Location of Brazil", author Salman Rushdie describes a whole new race, created by mass migrations, of "… people who root themselves in ideas rather than places, in memories as much as in material things".[2]

**What makes a place feel like home?**

Personal history, roots and memories connect us to those homes that are part of our identity, the homes where our family history is found, the homes where we belong. Sometimes, however, places just click, even though we have not spent much time there. Cultural fit is a term used mostly in a business context, but also is appropriate for describing how well our personality fits with the values, norms and behaviours of a culture. The better the cultural fit, the more at home we feel.

If we perceive that a society's core values and beliefs are close to our own, then we are likely to feel more comfortable, relaxed and safe – and this will help with adjustment. Similarly, if a culture values certain aspects of our personality, we are likely to feel a stronger sense of belonging in that culture. Finally, familiarity with a country's language has the same effect – of making us feel psychologically safe. One study[3] found that the greater the contrast between geographies, languages, customs, values and habits (what the authors of the study call 'cultural complexity'), the more effort it takes to adjust and the more skills we need to bring to the table.

Understanding how the people around us think and behave also creates a feeling of home. Paula, a lively Brazilian in her mid-forties, talks about understanding the 'Code' of a culture as "understanding the way people function, how they talk and what they talk about, what they find funny." Each culture has its own Code. If we know the Code, we know how the society works – the mentality, the social norms, the values – and that gives us a sense of belonging. When she first moved to Vienna, Paula felt like a foreigner because she didn't know the Code. After ten years of living there, "I get it much more, although I still don't have it. I still don't get all the jokes here. In Brazil, when people are talking next to me, I know what they are talking about, even if they whisper. I can read their facial expressions and interpret their gestures. Understanding the Code makes me feel at home."

**What are the feelings that home evokes?**

Home is belonging, feeling accepted and welcome. Home is also feeling safe and secure. For many of us, home is our refuge, our safe haven. Being home means knowing that we can let down our guard and find peace of mind. Norma McCaig,[4] founder of the organization Global Nomads International, talks about an 'internal home' of memories and emotions collected over time from which we draw comfort and strength, when needed: "It's as if we [global nomads] have replaced the physical home of non-nomads … with an internal home we can go to when we need a respite from the world."[5]

My research shows that the more mobile our lives are, the more important our internal home becomes. Home is a feeling of comfort. It can be the comfort of familiarity in your environment – knowing how to get around or get things done. Or it can be a comfort of authenticity – being ourselves and feeling accepted for who we are.

Authenticity can be linked to the ability to communicate through language. Many expats claim that their personalities are different in different languages. Like Isabel, a vibrant Spaniard living in Lausanne, who asserts: "I am a different version of myself in French. In Spanish, I am extroverted and lively, while in French, I am much more hesitant and subdued." Often, this inability to be authentic in a language stands in the way of feeling at home. This explains why, as expats, we may often seek out people who speak our language. As we assemble, disassemble and reassemble our life multiple times, we can sometimes lose track of the core of who we are. When we are able to be ourselves, we are able to feel at home. Many of us, despite our multicultural lives, can only be genuine in one language. So, we seek out people who speak our language because it feels good to be ourselves from time to time.

Finally, the feeling of home can be found in a single moment, a picture, a smell, an event that moves us – sharing a meal with our loved ones, or sitting on a deserted beach listening to the waves crash on the shore. In his book *The Global Soul*, Pico Iyer writes of a man for whom "the only home he knew ... had come in two unexpected moments of stillness – spiritual epiphanies, really – while travelling through rural Ireland."[6]

## HOME AS PEOPLE

I lived in Vienna for 11 years prior to moving to Zurich. For years, I felt disconnected and homeless, until I found the people who became my home, friends who became so dear to me that they were like family. Because of them, Vienna became home. When we moved away, it was this home-as-people that I missed.

Being among the people we love makes us feel grounded. It gives us all the ingredients of home – comfort, security, love, belonging. The more we move around and the more rootless our lives become, the likelier some of us are to seek roots in people rather than places and find home in relationships rather than material things. This relational home stays with us wherever we are. Often, we can't control *where* we live, but we can control *with whom* we live. The people in our lives are the home we choose.

### Who are the people who become our home?

First, of course, is our family. Moving together intensifies bonds within the nuclear family. Family becomes the only constant point of reference when everything around us changes. It provides a sense of security, stability and continuity when there is no physical base that can do that. Almost everyone I interviewed mentioned family as a primary dimension of home.

David, a Canadian whose family moved almost every year during his early childhood, considers family to be a key element of his identity. "Because of my history, family is one of the main pillars of my life. It was the only constant element when I was growing up and became my concept of home. I was reluctant to invest in friendships, knowing that, inevitably, I would lose them when I moved. Instead, I centred myself around my family, because it provided me with the stability and continuity that I needed. There was always a new house, a new school, a new environment, but my family was my anchor through all the tumult." David moved to the US as a young adult, where he met an American, married her and started a family. At some point, the family moved to Europe, to pursue a job opportunity for David. His childhood experience shaped the way he approached that move. "I had the same concept of home in mind as in my childhood moves – the assumption that as long as the family stayed together, everything would be fine. This awareness kept our family together through the changes and we had a very strong bonding experience."

Besides family, close friends also contribute to our feeling of home. This is especially true for those of us who move alone. As we leave our anchor points back home, the friendships we create become our new anchors. The community we build with every move allows us to regain a sense of belonging. This community, our 'tribe', is a fundamental element of expat life. They are our friends, neighbours, colleagues, fellow students, friends of friends. They are the people with whom we can be ourselves. They understand how we think and feel, even if we don't know each other very long.

For many of us global nomads, other global nomads are our tribe. Despite coming from different backgrounds and native languages or different generations, we naturally gravitate towards each other. We understand each other and connect much more than we do with people whose national identity and concept of home are clearly defined. Finding our tribe as expats helps us survive homesickness and homelessness. It helps us find our home.

## HOME IS EVERYWHERE AND NOWHERE

While foundational for many, the concepts of home as place, feeling or people do not apply to everyone. For some, home is everywhere; for others, nowhere. For still others, it is both everywhere and nowhere at the same time. Global nomads are used to the foreigner's dilemma: the internal divide, the permanent tension between the places they leave behind and the ones ahead of them. They are used to constantly negotiating a balance between different worlds and ways of life, feeling close to many cultures, but not identifying fully with any of them, being outsiders. These 'global souls' are in-betweeners, children of blurred boundaries and global mobility, resident aliens of the world, impermanent residents of nowhere.[7]

Arianna, a native of Cyprus, calls people who, like her, have lost the ability to 'fit in' in any one culture, 'insider-outsiders'. Arianna left home when she was 18 to go to university in the US. More than ten years and a few university degrees later, she and her Cypriot husband – whom she met in the US – decided to return to Cyprus. Arianna, who had been reluctant to move back, had a hard time adjusting. "I don't feel at home in either place," she says. "I don't belong here, but when I visit my friends in the US, I'm an outsider there too." Arianna does not regret being an 'insider-outsider', because it is the price to pay for being able to enjoy the privileges of a global life. "I might have been happier had I been more integrated here – reading the local papers, watching the Greek sitcoms on TV and eating *souvla* [a typical Cypriot dish] every day. But I wouldn't know better. I have learned to be comfortable with the discomfort of being 'in between' because I find room for creativity and change in that discomfort. Being on the periphery, I learn more. I gain more. And I do more."

Do all expats experience not belonging as a discomfort? Not everyone places home at the core of their identity.

Some do not need that kind of grounding and are happy not to settle anywhere. They cherish the opportunity to get to know and be influenced by different cultures. They appreciate the broader perspectives. They find permanence undesirable and confusing, rootlessness enriching and liberating. Rootlessness can also be seen as the blessing of multiple homes. We accumulate homes over time – whether they are linked to place, people, values, memories or experiences. These homes are all part of who we are. We belong to all of them, even if we don't belong to any single one of them.

Even as we appreciate freedom from affiliation, we still get homesick. Homesickness is an enduring feature of human life, even in its new mobile, cosmopolitan version. We declare that the world is our home, but our philosophy is not always in harmony with our emotions. Despite modern transportation and communication technologies that reduce the sense of distance and create the illusion of home being close at hand, homesickness has not disappeared from the range of human emotions. All these advances are "the next best thing to being there, but they are not the same as being there."[8] Not having a home can be stressful and exhausting.

In her book *Homesickness*, Susan Matt writes, referring to modern-day America: "… it is clear that we still live in the midst of a homesick culture. All across the country are signs of people dealing with the changes brought on by mobility, longing for someplace else, for family, for connections with what they have left behind."[9] One only has to look at studies of immigrant populations to establish that. A 2012 study published in the academic journal *Archives of General Psychiatry* found that Mexican immigrants in the US had rates of depression and anxiety 40% higher than non-migrant relatives remaining in Mexico. Several other studies document higher rates of depression and 'acculturative stress' among other groups of new immigrants to the US.[10]

## CONCEPT OF HOME

Why is it important to understand your concept of home? Your quest for home and the kind of home you look for affect how you manage transitions to new places. They influence the coping strategies, conscious or subconscious, that you use to approach each phase of a move – from deciding whether and where to move, to planning and preparing the move, moving and, finally, settling into your new home.

How much do your positive and not-so-positive experiences of moving have to do with your concepts of home? How do these concepts fit with where you live? Do you address them explicitly when you create a new home? I believe that becoming more aware of your core concepts of home can help you find home wherever you are, and to transition more easily through the stages of adjustment as you move.

## FINDING HOME

For those of us for whom home is place, nomadic life can be challenging. Letting go of places is difficult by definition. We long for the physical elements of home, the stretch of beach on which we played as children, the sounds of the neighbourhood where we grew up, the smells of our favourite foods. Still, just because home is place does not mean that you cannot make successful moves. Being aware of your geographical concept of home can help you devise strategies for approaching the different phases of the moving process.

When home is more feeling than place, you need first to clarify what that feeling consists of. Is it having a safe haven? Feeling loved and accepted for who you are? Having a sense of belonging? Being clear about the emotional dimensions of home will help you find ways to recreate that home wherever you are.

When home is people, start by determining what relationships are at the core of your concept of home. For expats, these relationships are often spread out geographically and over time – they are bonds from your past and your present, across all the places that matter to you. Clarity about the people who make home for you will guide you to find home wherever you are.

Susan, an American former expat, grew up in the rural Midwest of the United States. She describes her hometown as "a place where you talked loud, lived big and worked hard with your hands." Susan, a quiet and reflective person, never felt that she fit in the extroverted culture she was born into. After graduating from college, she got a job in Tokyo, Japan, and moved there. While, as an American, she was a cultural outsider, her introverted self – the self that didn't fit in back home – felt perfectly at home in Japan. The Japanese culture embraced and valued her reflective side. Susan told me a story from her first few weeks in Tokyo that illustrates the subtleties of creating home in new places. One evening, she had gone out with some friends and, on her way home at the end of the evening, she took the wrong train. She was not yet entirely familiar with Tokyo's public transport system and, by the time she realized her mistake, she had to get off in the middle of nowhere in the Japanese countryside. It was late at night and there were no more trains going back to Tokyo, so she had to wait for the first morning train. She sat for several hours, in her short skirt, high heels and tired makeup in the middle of winter, until it started to get light. She watched the dawn break over a grassy field. "It was a magical moment," she said. "After growing up in the rural Midwest, busy, overcrowded Tokyo was the exact opposite of home for me. But, as I stood there watching the sun rise over the Japanese fields and country houses, I had a profound feeling of home." Reflecting on that experience, she realized that understanding her deep need for nature and the outdoors, and using that concept of home as a guide, would help her find home anywhere in the world.

Home, whether it is a place, a feeling, people or a combination of these, is at the core of our identity. It has a powerful influence on our behaviour and the choices we make. A deep understanding of what home means is the foundation of every successful move. It helps us make sense of what happens to us during such transitions, and it guides the way we approach every moment and every aspect of the different stages of transition. After all, isn't a move a quest for home, a constant process of creating, dismantling and recreating home? In the chapters that follow, I will demonstrate the powerful influence of home on how we manage every phase of a move.

## CHECKLIST

- If you have moved in the past, what are some ways you have tried to create home in a new location? What has worked and what hasn't?

- Which of the concepts of home – as place, as feeling, as people or a combination – seems to fit you best? Why is that the case?

- Has your concept of home changed over time or remained largely the same? If it has changed, how and why?

- How would a deeper understanding of your concept(s) of home help you make your move easier?

- What can you do to understand more about your core concept(s) of home?

**PRINCIPLE #2:**
THE PROCESS OF
TRANSITION MATTERS

*"There's a classic curve at two to three months, when the excitement has died down and people find themselves in this hole ... after seven or eight months, people tend to start feeling at home again. Knowing that this will come and that it happens to a lot of people should help you get through it."*

**Simon Kuper,** "Moving Experiences"

When we moved to Zurich, my oldest son, who was ten years old and had lived only in Vienna until then, had a hard time adjusting. He was the new kid at school, did not speak Swiss German, felt like he didn't fit in and missed his friends. At some point it got so bad, he even asked to change schools. He kept insisting that the only thing that would make him happy would be to move back to Vienna, the only home he had known. He became deeply sad, and sometimes even angry – at his father, because he took the job that moved us away from our home in Austria, and at me, for agreeing to move.

One evening, as I was kissing him goodnight, I mentioned the stages of adjustment that I was familiar with from my research.

"Look," I told him, drawing an imaginary line with my finger on the wall next to his bed, "here is the 'U-curve' of adjustment. You start on a high when you arrive to a new place. Everything is new and exciting. Then you go through a crisis. You feel overwhelmed and sad. You miss your previous home. See, that's the bottom of the curve. And then, eventually, you recover and even start to feel at home in the new place. See here, at a point more or less as high as where you started. I've been through these stages myself several times, every time I moved."

His eyes widened (my son loves structure). "So where am I right now?" He traced his fingers over the imaginary U-curve. I pointed to the bottom of the curve.

"And this is where I will be later?" He pointed to the top. I nodded. "Okay," he said, and snuggled beneath the covers.

From that day, his complaints lessened, his sadness lightened, and he started to see things more positively.

According to a survey by HSBC, most adults (67%) say that it takes more than six months to feel at home in their new country, with 49% saying it takes more than a year. Some 48% of parents say that their children also need longer than six months, with 25% saying that they take more than a year to go through the whole transition cycle.[1]

Moving is a challenging process for both adults and children, and while some find it easier to cope than others, it takes time. Challenges include missing family and friends back home, adjusting to a new living space, learning a new language, settling into a new school, and making new friends.

Moving to a new place is a process of transition and adaptation. Although the exact sequence of events may differ for each of us, research shows that we tend to go through the same or similar stages every time we move, a relatively predictable series of ups and downs, regardless of the circumstances of the move. Each of the stages of adjustment has its own challenges.

An awareness of this process of transition and adaptation is fundamental for making a successful move because it increases our ability to manage the ups and downs and cope with culture shock. As was the case for my son, knowing what's coming is not only comforting, but it also allows us to anticipate and address the difficulties likely to come up and get appropriate support. If you expect it, you can prepare mentally and plan for it.

## THE STAGES OF ADJUSTMENT

Anthropologist Kalervo Oberg coined the term 'culture shock' in the 1950s to describe the collection of stressful feelings that build up when people enter a new culture and try to adjust to it. These feelings include confusion, disorientation, anxiety, frustration, incompetence and powerlessness. Culture shock is a consistent feature of expat life. When we enter a new culture, we leave behind familiar surroundings and cultural assumptions and have to adapt to new ones that may differ from or contradict what we've been used to.

A substantial amount of research has been done on the stages of culture shock (also referred to as stages of adjustment, cultural adaptation or expatriate adjustment over time). While the names given to each stage differ, the characteristics are similar. I will present here one of the most widely known models: the four stages of the U-curve theory of adjustment to culture shock.[2]

### Stage 1: Honeymoon

When Sofia first arrived in a small town of 21,000 inhabitants in Nebraska as an exchange student, she felt like she was part of one of those American teenage series she'd been watching on TV back in her hometown, Madrid. "It was like holidays for me. I had so much fun in the beginning. All these things that I saw in the movies but didn't know really existed, they were all there – cheerleaders, homecoming and all."

Sofia was the highlight of the town. Everybody talked about her. Everybody wanted to meet her. She was even mentioned in the local paper: "SPANISH GIRL COMING TO OUR TOWN!" She was excited about meeting new people and experiencing a new culture.

During the honeymoon stage, which can last anywhere from a few days to weeks or even months, everything is new and interesting. You are fascinated by your new environment and culture, excited about the possibilities, and eager to discover and experience everything. You associate with locals, who may make an effort to speak your language and are welcoming and polite to you as a foreigner. You are out of the ordinary and interesting to them. If you feel some stress, you tend to interpret it positively. You have the mindset of a tourist: you are observing, rather than becoming deeply involved in the new culture. Sofia loved the attention, but for her, it only lasted two months.

## Stage 2: Crisis

For Jasmine, a Lebanese expat, moving to Zurich was the first time she had left London, the place where she grew up. Though her family came from Beirut, where she was born (a city she hardly remembered), London had always been home. After a couple months in Zurich, and even though she liked the city a lot, she was miserable. She missed her family, her friends, her routines, and the smells, sounds and colours of home.

"I had just settled in Zurich, a city of a little more than 300,000 inhabitants, who spoke a language that was completely foreign to me (I hadn't even *heard* of Swiss German until then), when it hit me: 'Oh my God, what have I done?' Nothing was familiar. I found nothing that I could relate to. For the first few months, I would pack my bags every day and tell my husband: 'That's it. I'm leaving. I'm going back home.' My parents would call me from London, pleading with me not to leave Zurich – and my husband, whose career brought us there. To try to console me, every few months he would buy me a ticket to visit my parents."

After a few weeks or months in a new place, you are no longer a tourist, nor are you regarded as one. Routine sets in, and with it, disillusionment. You miss your old life and sense of home. The differences between the old and the new culture seem stark and uncomfortable, creating anxiety. Things start to go wrong. Perhaps you struggle to communicate in the new language. You are less fascinated and more irritated. You lament the (genuine) difficulties that you face, often turning to the company of people from your home culture with similar experiences. You feel homesick and isolated, stressed and perhaps even depressed. During that first year, every time Jasmine came back from a visit to London, it would take her a week to recover.

## Stage 3: Recovery

Andrea, another Canadian expat, made her first international move in her mid-30s, from Montreal to Paris. Eighteen months into her stay there, and having gone through both honeymoon and crisis, Andrea fell in love with France when she and her family moved to a suburb on the outskirts of the city. "I finally settled there. I knew how things worked. I had a family doctor. I made friends, both expats and French people. I built a support system for our family. I started feeling at home. I found 'my' people, developed my routines and became part of a community."

If you overcome the crisis phase and stay on, you eventually reach the recovery stage, which feels like a breakthrough, because suddenly things start to make sense. You begin to feel comfortable and learn how to function effectively in your new environment: you get around without getting lost, develop routines, get things done, understand what's going on around you, even start giving advice to newcomers. You connect with people and feel less isolated. You get better at reading cultural values and cues, and more tolerant (and even appreciative) of local habits. Things that previously seemed unbearable bother you less. You still feel irritated and stressed at times, but you address those feelings more positively. Andrea did not stop feeling like a foreigner when she moved to that Parisian suburb. She still got frustrated on a regular basis, but overall, she felt more accepted and at ease.

## Stage 4: Adjustment

After a little more than a year in Vienna, Paula, a Brazilian expat, felt integrated in her new home. "I learned to go with the flow. I started accepting that things are a certain way and got used to them. I started to notice the good things Vienna could give me. For example, it's such a safe and beautiful city and there is always something interesting to do, especially with the kids. Every day can be an adventure, if one wants. When my tears were gone, I was able to see the beauty."

In this final stage of the adjustment process, you begin to feel at home. You accept reality and start to enjoy it. You appreciate the differences between the old and the new culture and come to terms with the latter. You are able to function, live and work with confidence and ease in your new environment. While you may feel strained sometimes, you are not in a state of constant anxiety like in the crisis stage. For Paula, adjustment was linked to letting go. It came when she stopped comparing her new life in Vienna to her old one in Brazil.

The following graphic of the U-curve of cross-cultural adjustment illustrates how wellbeing evolves over time, as one progresses through each of these stages:

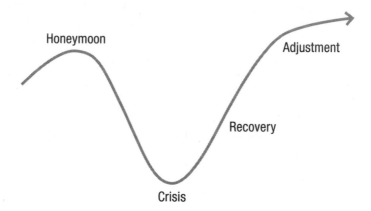

**Figure 2.1: The U-Curve of Cross-Cultural Adjustment**

Source: http://www.missouristate.edu/advising/international/160467.htm

## ACCELERATING ADJUSTMENT

In practice, the process of adaptation is not as linear and clear-cut as the stages of the U-curve theory I just described (or other theories about the stages) may make us think. In fact, there is not one single pattern of adjustment. Neither the duration nor the sequence of the stages is set in stone. Stages may not follow one another sequentially. They may blend or overlap. Or they may vary in length for different people or in different situations. Some may not experience all four stages or may experience some stages more than once. For example, they may move from crisis to adjustment and then suddenly a new event may bring on a new crisis, which may set the process back. Each person goes through their own unique process.

The reasons people often differ in the magnitude and duration of their adjustment experiences are linked to differences in personality, family situation, preparation, assignment circumstances or other factors. You may have an easier time adjusting to cultures that fit better with your personality. Or moving with a supportive spouse or a partner that is already familiar with the host culture may speed up your adjustment.

The adaptation experience may also look very different than the stages described above for those who don't want to move, yet have to follow. A spouse, partner or child who feels like they have no choice but to move may go through an initial process that looks more like grieving than honeymoon. They may go through at least some of the stages of grief, such as shock and denial, anger, bargaining, even depression, before reaching acceptance and opening themselves up to the adjustment process.[3] It is important to acknowledge this grief and allow time and space for the grieving process to take place, in order to be able to move on to adjustment.

Despite all the caveats, being aware of the classic pattern of adjustment is an invaluable guide for navigating transitions, for practical but also emotional reasons. The framework is a tool to help you identify and understand what you may be feeling and why. And let us not forget that adjustment is an ongoing process.

Finally, although culture shock may affect some of us more or in different ways than it affects others, the fact that we get culture shock at all is linked to a deep need and constant quest for home. As Maya Angelou said, "The ache for home lives in all of us." We go through all these stages in order to find home.

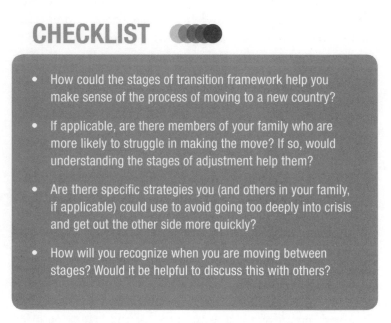

## CHECKLIST

- How could the stages of transition framework help you make sense of the process of moving to a new country?

- If applicable, are there members of your family who are more likely to struggle in making the move? If so, would understanding the stages of adjustment help them?

- Are there specific strategies you (and others in your family, if applicable) could use to avoid going too deeply into crisis and get out the other side more quickly?

- How will you recognize when you are moving between stages? Would it be helpful to discuss this with others?

# 3

## PRINCIPLE #3:
YOU MATTER

*"It is not the strongest of the species that survive,
nor the most intelligent,
but the one most responsive to change."*

**Charles Darwin**

Shira is getting ready to meet her husband Roger at a new bar that just opened on the banks of the Rhine. She's not looking forward to the night out. Roger spontaneously had invited a colleague and her husband who are new in town to join them for drinks. *Typical Roger,* she thinks, *playing the role of welcoming committee for newcomers.*

Shira and Roger had moved to Basel from the US less than two years earlier. He's Swiss, from the French side (and, like most Swiss, also fluent in German), and she's Israeli. This is not Shira's first move abroad, which makes it even more surprising that it has taken her so long to get her bearings.

Shira is annoyed that Roger didn't consult with her before committing to go out. She had a long day at work, and they had agreed to stay in tonight. As an introvert, she needs her time and space to recharge. When she does go out, she prefers to spend time with her small circle of good friends. Roger, however, loves meeting new people. He is curious and genuinely interested. He is also spontaneous and energized by not knowing what comes next. Shira prefers structure and planning, and does not appreciate last-minute changes. She sighs as she puts the final touches on her makeup, picks up her purse and heads out.

To make a successful move, it helps to understand how our personal characteristics affect the way we adapt to changes in our life circumstances. Shira and Roger have very different personalities and life experiences, so they respond to change in very different ways. This had a profound impact on how they experienced their move to Switzerland. Had they been more aware of their differences (and their impact), Shira would have had an easier time adjusting, and there would have been less tension between them.

Shira, the introvert, takes longer to adjust to new circumstances than Roger, the extrovert. When they first moved to Basel, she was intensely lonely and overwhelmed. She missed her family and felt isolated. Although she spoke some German, she wasn't fluent like Roger and hesitated to use it to communicate. She experienced the cultural change – both compared to what she grew up with and her previous life in the US – as massive and shocking. It took two years in Basel before she was able to create that small circle of close friends with whom she liked to socialize. Fortunately, the Swiss cultural affinity for timely planning worked well for her, helping her maintain a sense of control over building her support network.

In addition to being an extrovert, Roger is more open to new experiences than Shira. While she prefers to spend a lot of time at home, he enjoys going out and meeting new people. He relishes novelty and new opportunities. He goes with the flow. Knowing how his wife struggles to make new connections, he takes it upon himself to organize their social agenda and makes an effort to introduce her to the spouses of colleagues or other people he thinks she'll find interesting. He often thinks that, if both he and Shira had been introverts, they would have had an even harder time adjusting to new places. Even so, their different speeds of adaptation sometimes create tension between them.

While personalities are very important, experience and the skills we acquire over time also play a role in the adjustment process. Shira spent most of her childhood and early adulthood in one place and had moved only once before their move to Switzerland. As a child of a diplomat, Roger had moved every three to four years. As a result, he developed skills for dealing with change, including a strong sense of resilience and an eagerness to learn new things. "There wasn't much reward for becoming attached to places or people, because there was so much moving around and also, I guess, some disappointments. This may sound negative, but I also see the positive side. It made me curious and restless, so that the prospect of moving someplace new is much more energizing to me than the idea of staying put."

Because of his highly mobile childhood, Roger also developed the ability to create connections easily. "In both physical places and relationships, I can quickly develop a sense of intimacy and closeness. I make very close friends very quickly by most people's standards and feel at home also relatively quickly, even if I know it is transient."

While there is no 'perfect expat' profile, studies have shown that there are personal qualities that help accelerate the adjustment process: openness, extraversion, flexibility, cultural sensitivity and resilience, among others. These are the result of a mix of innate personality traits and acquired abilities developed through experience and learning. Together, personality and experience have a powerful influence on how people deal with transitions. While your personality has a substantial impact, your life history and circumstances (for instance, whether you have spent your whole childhood moving around or only embarked on your first international posting as an adult) can also influence the skills you develop, making you more (or less) 'fit' for expat life.

The more aware you are of your characteristics, the easier it becomes to navigate the move. Of course, the line between innate personality traits and acquired abilities can be blurry. For instance, is flexibility a quality one is born with or is it developed as a result of specific life experiences? The answer, often, is both. Regardless, as you navigate a move, it is important to take stock of your strengths and vulnerabilities, as they have a powerful influence on how you cope in different transition situations. The good news is that, even if you do not have all the traits, skills and abilities you will read about in the sections that follow, you can learn and develop many of them.

## THE IMPACT OF YOUR PERSONALITY

What is the structure of your personality and how will it help or hinder you in making a successful move? Numerous studies have examined the relationship between personality traits and success on corporate expatriate assignments, which, of course, is strongly linked to success in adjusting to foreign environments. Virtually all of these studies are aimed at the corporate world and are driven by the imperative to select the 'right' employees for international postings, that is, the ones most likely to thrive and deliver outstanding business results.

### The Structure of Personality

After decades of research, organizational psychologists converged on what is known as the 'Big Five' personality traits. These are considered to be the building blocks of personality and are summarized with the acronym OCEAN:

1. **Openness to experience**: The tendency to be curious and non-judgemental, and to embrace, rather than fear, change.
2. **Conscientiousness**: The tendency to be organized, self-disciplined and dependable.
3. **Extraversion**: The tendency to seek stimulation and derive energy from the company of others.
4. **Agreeableness**: The tendency to be friendly, compassionate and cooperative.
5. **Neuroticism**: The tendency to experience negative emotions easily, for instance, anger, anxiety or depression (the opposite of neuroticism is Emotional Stability).

## Openness

If you are open to new experiences, as Roger was, then you are intellectually curious, interested in the world and keen to learn, also from your mistakes. You are not attached to any established way of doing things. You cope well with change because you are more accepting of new environments or cultures than someone who is conservative and resistant to novelty. All that makes you adaptable. Openness also tends to make you more tolerant. You tend to accept people as they are and not judge them. That makes it easier for you create friendships when you move to a new place, which, in turn, increases your chances of understanding and becoming comfortable in the new culture. Again, all that has a positive impact on your adjustment.

## Conscientiousness

If you score high on conscientiousness, you tend to like routines and rituals. They bring structure to your life and help you adjust faster. You usually are good at setting goals, planning and creating support structures. At the same time, taken to its extreme, your love of structure may make you more rigid and less willing (or able) to deal with ambiguity and uncertainty, to let go or to accept imperfect outcomes. All that may make adjustment more challenging.

## Extraversion

We saw earlier how Roger and Shira were on the two extremes of the intro-/extroversion spectrum and how that affected their adjustment. If you're an extrovert, like Roger, you find it easier to start conversations with complete strangers or to practice speaking languages you're just starting to learn. You are more likely to socialize and make friends easily, because you find it energizing. As a result, you may be able to integrate into a new culture faster and better than an introvert would. If you're an introvert, like Shira, you are most likely better at building deeper, long-lasting connections that will allow you to feel grounded in your new environment.

**Agreeableness**
A pleasant, friendly and positive attitude is key to helping you build your local social and support system early on in your transition process – and therefore lessen the stress of adjustment. Both Roger and Shira were on the more agreeable side of the spectrum, which helped them get connected and feel at home, albeit at different speeds. If you are somewhere on the less agreeable end, this does not necessarily mean that you will have a hard time adjusting, but you might have to put in more effort to compensate for it.

**Neuroticism**
This is the only trait where scoring *low*, rather than high, is positively associated with adjustment. The lower you score on neuroticism, the more emotionally stable you are, and the more you tend to see things positively, including the inevitable ups and downs of relocation. That predisposition makes you better equipped to cope with setbacks and challenges. Scoring high on neuroticism makes you less emotionally stable, more susceptible to external pressures, and likelier to view temporary setbacks as permanent conditions. This can make it harder to cope with stress and the challenges of cross-cultural adjustment.

## Assessing Yourself
There are many psychometric instruments available that measure the Big Five, including the Newcastle Personality Assessor,[1] Facet5[2] and the NEO.[3] For an informal way to get a quick sense of where you stand, complete **Figure 3.1** on the next page.

## Figure 3.1: Big Five Informal Diagnostic Tool

Where do you position yourself along the following scales?
Circle the responses that best fit you.

**Openness**
How open are you to new experiences?

| Not at all | Somewhat | Average | Substantially | I love change |
|---|---|---|---|---|
| 1 | 2 | 3 | 4 | 5 |

**Conscientiousness**
How high is your ability and need for structure and organization?

| Low | | Average | | High |
|---|---|---|---|---|
| 1 | 2 | 3 | 4 | 5 |

**Extraversion**
How extroverted/introverted are you?

| Introverted | | Mid-Range | | Extroverted |
|---|---|---|---|---|
| 1 | 2 | 3 | 4 | 5 |

**Agreeableness**
How would you rate your tendency to be friendly,
compassionate and cooperative?

| Low | | Average | | High |
|---|---|---|---|---|
| 1 | 2 | 3 | 4 | 5 |

**Neuroticism**
How likely are you to experience negative emotions? The less
often you do, the more emotionally stable you are.

| All the time | Often | Sometimes | Rarely | Never |
|---|---|---|---|---|
| 1 | 2 | 3 | 4 | 5 |

Your position on these scales will tend to influence in what way, and how rapidly, you adapt to new cultures. Scoring high (i.e., on the right side of each scale) is associated with better cross-cultural adjustment. Studies show that those who are open, structured, extroverted and emotionally balanced adjust more easily to new cultures, compared to those at the other end of the spectrum with respect to the Big Five traits.[4] Furthermore, scoring high on agreeableness has been found to have a positive influence on both expat adjustment and job performance.[5]

It's not hard to understand why these associations make intuitive sense, and you should think about the implications for your own adjustment after a move. Our personalities are, of course, more complex than these five traits, and we are not taking into account the complexity of interactions among traits. Also, many of us are somewhere in the middle of each spectrum, not at the extremes. One final caveat here is that cultures differ widely in the degrees of appreciation for different personality traits, so adjustment and effectiveness may also vary depending on the interaction between traits and the culture of a particular society. That said, the Big Five remains a useful framework for understanding the impact of personality on cross-cultural adjustment.

## CULTIVATING ADAPTIVE ABILITIES

If you are not on the 'easy adjuster' end of the Big Five personality scales, don't give up hope. It helps a great deal to understand if and why your personality may cause you to have difficulties adjusting, as it will help you anticipate and get appropriate support. Focus on taking an inventory of the adaptive traits you already possess and those you need to cultivate.

Brigit grew up in a small seaside town in Norway. She was an introvert and not particularly open to change. However, her adaptability increased dramatically when, at the age of 19, she enrolled in a Folk High School,[6] a type of boarding school a few hours from home. There, she spent a year living and studying with young people from all over the world. As a result, she developed a strong sense of cross-cultural awareness and learned how to adapt to a much broader set of people and circumstances. She went on to study at university in Oslo, where she met her husband Sven. Soon after their marriage, Sven was accepted to a PhD program at Berkeley, in California, so they decided to move.

Despite her brand-new master's degree, Brigit's visa did not allow her to work in the US, at least not in a paid position. "All my friends from university had started working already and they were writing to me and expressing their excitement. I was really eager to work and felt that I had all these skills and was ready to use what I'd learned for so long ... and I just couldn't because of my visa. That was incredibly frustrating in the beginning, but then I thought to myself, *how do I deal with these restrictions the best I can?* I am in a field where there are plenty of opportunities, even if I don't get paid. I should take advantage of that. So, I started doing volunteer work."

Brigit decided to volunteer at the international office at Berkeley as a welcoming liaison for the spouses of students. Soon enough, she realized that there was a strong need for information, ranging from legal and procedural (like how to get a driver's license) to resources for emotional and psychological support. She started writing a handbook for international spouses. One day, talking to one of her colleagues, she found out about a refugee shelter nearby and volunteered there as well.

"I found so much meaning in helping others. Suddenly, I found this purpose I had been missing. When I moved to California as a spouse and homemaker, I was missing a large part of my identity, and I finally got it back."

Eventually, Brigit obtained a visa and was hired by the university. "[Through my experiences at the Folk High School,] I learned that you have to be flexible and patient and not expect things to just happen for you. You take advantage of the opportunities that are there, instead of lamenting the ones that you have lost."

Like Brigit, your personality is not the end of the story in terms of how you cope with transitions in expat life. Skills and abilities that you acquire over the course of your life can have an impact on how well you adapt to new cultures. The following characteristics are, of course, somewhat shaped by personality, but there is much you can do to develop them.

## Flexibility and Resilience

You can be born with a tendency to be more open to experience and therefore more flexible. Like Brigit, however, you can start on the low side and develop it during the course of your life, because of the way you are raised, the role models provided by your parents, your early experiences and your positive decisions to become more flexible.

When you move abroad, you are constantly confronted with change: new situations, new people, new cultural values, attitudes and behaviours. What is your relationship to change? Do you resist it, see it as disruptive, stressful and a source of anxiety? Or do you embrace it and see it as a natural part of life and a learning opportunity? Flexibility is exactly that: the ability to accept change, to 'roll with the punches' and make the most of every new situation. It's the ability to let go of your past life and thrive in your new one. As a result of her experience at the Folk High School, Brigit consciously decided to focus on the opportunities rather than the constraints of her situation in the US. She thought about how she could make the most of her current circumstances, acted upon it and ended up with a solid sense of purpose, contribution and achievement.

Flexibility also implies tolerance for ambiguity. If you want everything to be as it was back home, then relocation will be a tough experience because you can never recreate exactly what you had. Think of small lifestyle changes and how you deal with them. You may be used to driving your car everywhere and suddenly have to rely exclusively on public transport because the traffic is so bad. Or, like Linda, a visual artist from New York, who moved to a small village in Central America to work with local farming communities, you may enter your new home and realise that it has no kitchen sink, toilet or other indoor plumbing. While it's essential to plan and implement your plan well, expat life has its way of teaching you to let go of the need to control everything. Being willing and able to deal with lack of structure and routine, at least temporarily, will help you immensely as you navigate transition and adjustment.

Resilience is related to flexibility. It's the ability to manage stress without breaking down. Given that stress is inherent in making international moves, resilience is a key 'good expat' quality. It helps to understand what it is about the experience of moving that creates stress. The answer lies in understanding our fundamental drivers and how the expat experience affects them.

Research on motivation has revealed that people have three universal innate psychological needs that motivate most of our behaviour and are essential for our mental health and psychological wellbeing. While the relative importance varies from person to person (and is another component of personality), all three are important to some degree.[7]

1. **Autonomy** – The need to have control over our life, be free to set goals and make choices;
2. **Achievement** – The desire to have an impact on our environment, to learn and further our personal growth; and
3. **Affiliation** - The need to have intimate, loving relationships and a feeling of belonging to a community.

Moving to a new culture diminishes our ability to fulfil these three needs, at least at the beginning. When we move, we may feel as if we have much less control over our own lives.

We may find ourselves less able to achieve than in our familiar environment: we are not comfortable in the new language; we don't understand the culture or how things are done in the new place. We may feel lonely and disconnected. As a result, we may get the sense that our life lacks meaning and direction, that we have lost part of our identity or that we are not motivated to do anything meaningful. This happens because one or more of our basic needs have been compromised by our new situation. The experience of adaptation is, in significant measure, about restoring those basic needs.

Resilience is the ability to cope with these challenges and to restore our sense of motivation in the face of setbacks. To be resilient means to be able to adapt to adversity, stress and changed circumstances, while maintaining physical and mental health and sustaining an accustomed level of energy. Being resilient also implies being able to maintain a positive attitude in most situations. It does not mean that you do not feel as much pain as others in your situation would. It means that you are better able to handle that pain and not let it overwhelm you and take over your life. Resilience is a state of mind. Do you conceptualize an event as traumatic, or as a chance to learn and grow?[8]

You can learn to be flexible and resilient.[9] Ways to do this include:

1. **Focus on accepting your situation.** Denial and resistance won't get you anywhere; they are impediments to adaptation. Strive to accept what you cannot control, so that you can focus on what you can control and find ways to cope.
2. **Find meaning in your situation.** Connect to your intention and find a purpose to keep you going when times are tough.
3. **Be creative.** Think outside the box. Make the most of what you have and open your mind to new possibilities.
4. **Visualize.** Picture what you want your ideal life to look like. Think of the different areas of your life, such as family,

personal development, career, social circle and others that are important to you. What do you want and what do you need to do to get there? Make your vision as specific and detailed as possible.

5. **Take action.** Go beyond acceptance. Counterintuitively, letting go and being accepting allows you to regain control over every new situation. Having a sense of control, even if it's over small things, such as your immediate environment, can be soothing and encouraging. Take small steps, focus your energy and believe in yourself.

6. **Don't do it alone.** While resilience is a personal quality, surrounding yourself with a supportive group of friends enhances that quality, makes life easier and helps you deal better with stress.

7. **Take care of yourself.** You cannot control stress, but you can choose how you react to it. Taking care of yourself – by eating well, sleeping enough, exercising and pursuing activities that relax and energize you – will give you the vitality and personal resources to tackle anything that life throws at you. Exercise has been shown to increase resilience.

8. **Maintain your sense of humour.** When faced with a stressful situation, try to gain some perspective and look at the big picture. Having a sense of humour increases immunity to stress and, of course, resilience.

## Culture and Language

Anna, a Dutch woman who grew up in Africa and lived in many different countries and continents as an adult, married a Slovenian man and eventually settled with him in Ljubljana, his hometown. In our interview, she talked about how living abroad helped her develop, over time, an awareness of and sensitivity to cultural differences.

"I find that living abroad equips you with so much more empathy for people with different backgrounds and cultures, than if you'd stayed in your home country. In my moves that translates, for example, into being conscious not to judge. If I am confronted with behaviour that could be interpreted as abrasive or even insulting, I always try to put it in context. I have become much more tolerant."

In a survey by the *Economist Intelligence Unit* (EIU), 73% of respondents selected cultural sensitivity as the most important attribute of a successful expatriate.[10] Other studies identified Cultural Intelligence (CQ) as an essential skill for working effectively in different cultural contexts.[11] Finally, another set of researchers studied intercultural or cross-cultural competence (IC) as a key skill for navigating different cultures.[12]

Regardless of the terms used (I will use 'cultural intelligence'), our ability to function effectively in different cultures is linked to how well we adapt through cross-cultural transitions.[13] High cultural intelligence does not come automatically, but everyone can develop it to some degree. By definition, it transcends specific cultures. It is a body of knowledge, skills and behaviours for making sense of the multitude of cultures we encounter. To be able to function effectively in a new culture, three elements need to be present at the same time: motivation (the willingness to learn and be effective), acquired knowledge (of the new culture, of your own cultural identity) and supporting skills (such as empathy and curiosity).

Learning about a new culture takes effort, so you have to be motivated, especially if you struggle to have the confidence to do so. When you find yourself interacting with people in an unfamiliar cultural setting, can you discipline yourself to try to see the world through their eyes? It takes effort, but it is possible to surmount the potential for discomfort in these situations.

A common definition of culture comes from Dutch social psychologist Geert Hofstede: "A collective programming of the mind that distinguishes the members of one group or category of people from another."[14] Culture consists of beliefs, core values, unwritten norms, rules and rituals, which are implicit, hard to measure and acquired over generations.

It strongly shapes behaviour. To be able to navigate a particular culture, you need to have a 'map' of that culture and how it influences behaviour.[15] This will provide information about how its people behave and what is expected of you to be part of that culture. Assuming you are willing (motivated), acquisition of this knowledge makes you able to see the world through the eyes of another culture.

The more rapidly you acquire knowledge about a specific culture, the more it helps you understand how cultures differ. There are several frameworks for understanding cultural differences. A well-known model developed by Hofstede identifies the following six dimensions of national culture:[16]

1. Power distance (hierarchical vs. more egalitarian societies).
2. Individualism vs. collectivism ('I' vs. 'we' societies).
3. Masculinity vs. femininity (preference for achievement and competitiveness vs. preference for modesty and cooperation).
4. Uncertainty avoidance (the degree to which the members of a society feel uncomfortable with uncertainty and ambiguity).
5. Long-term vs. short-term orientation (prioritizing links to time-honoured traditions and norms vs. prioritizing dealing with the challenges of the present and future).
6. Indulgence vs. restraint (a society that allows relatively free gratification of human needs vs. one that suppresses and regulates that by strict social norms).

A framework will also help you be aware of your own culture and understand how it differs from that of others. This awareness will allow you to consciously move beyond any biases in your cross-cultural encounters. As David Livermore, author of the book *The Cultural Intelligence Difference*, writes, "Biases are inevitable. Acting on them isn't."[17]

Skills that are important in developing cultural intelligence include empathy and curiosity. Here, too, personality and upbringing may constrain the extent to which empathy and curiosity can be developed. However, regardless of where you start, it is possible to develop those skills if you make a conscious effort to follow certain practices such as listening, suspending judgment and challenging prejudices, looking for commonalities and being vulnerable – all that, especially with people who are very different from you.

Then, there is language. Language and culture are inextricably connected. Language expresses culture and is shaped by it. How sensitive can you be and how well can you integrate into a new culture if you don't understand it or the people? If you truly want to experience a new place, language training is not a luxury. Simply understanding the cultural values and nuances hidden in the language can have a big impact on adjustment and social integration. The *Economist Intelligence Unit* survey also showed that willingness to learn a foreign language contributes strongly to having a positive expatriate experience and fully embracing its opportunities. This willingness is another indicator of, and contributor to, cultural sensitivity. And actually using the language matters too. Even if you don't fully master a foreign language, just by using it to communicate, you are likely to gain the respect of your counterparts.

When Linda, the visual artist from New York, moved to Central America, her knowledge of Spanish was minimal, but she was eager to learn. She found that the learning process itself accelerated her adaptation. "I wasn't thinking 'Oh my God, how will I learn Spanish?' but instead 'Of course, I will learn it!' A couple months of classes helped me feel more connected, and I found that people welcomed me with open arms. When you can't quite speak the language, communication becomes much more genuine: it's eye-to-eye, soul-to-soul, body-to-body. It takes you right to your core. I wish everyone would lose their tongue for a little while. It's the greatest gift in the world."

The longer you stay abroad, the more cultural diversity you confront and the better you learn to function in it.

Cross-cultural and language training can help you as well. If you want to be effective in a culturally diverse context, then you can work on and develop your skills in this area. Here are a few ways to build up your cultural intelligence:

1. **Be ready.** Be open to learning, willing to suspend your assumptions and value judgments, and prepared to adopt and function in multiple perspectives.
2. **Gather cultural knowledge**. Research, learn the language, meet people, observe and immerse yourself in the rituals and way of life as much as possible. The more you know, the easier it is to understand and accept.
3. **Understand your own culture and biases**. Take advantage of the opportunity to see your own culture through the eyes of those outside it.
4. **Be curious**. Don't hesitate to ask questions. Curiosity is the cornerstone of cultural intelligence and the first step that leads to the desire to gain knowledge.
5. **Develop your empathy**. Put yourself in others' shoes and try to see the world from their perspective.
6. **Take time to reflect on your experiences.**[18] Analyse things that happen to you, events and behaviours, from a cultural point of view. Dig deeper into their meaning. Extrapolate learnings for the future.

Use **Figure 3.2** to get a sense of where you stand in terms of the key 'expat skills' presented in the previous section.

Many of the skills that make a successful expat are learned on the field. You can develop, train and improve these traits consciously. The first step is to determine which abilities you need to develop. For that, you need to assess yourself – your personality traits and acquired skills – along the dimensions we explored. If possible, do this self-assessment before you even decide to move, so you have time to work on some of your weaker areas. Start with the set of diagnostic questions

## Figure 3.2: Adaptive Abilities Informal Diagnostic Tool

Where do you position yourself along the following scales?
Circle the responses that best fit you.

**Flexibility**
How would you rate your ability to go with the flow?

I need control                                                                                   Easy-going
--- 1 ----------- 2 ----------- 3 ----------- 4 ----------- 5 ---

**Resilience**
How would you rate your ability to bounce back from
adversity and stress?

    Low                          Average                         High
    1 ----------- 2 ----------- 3 ----------- 4 ----------- 5 ---

**Cultural Sensitivity**
How would you rate your ability to function effectively in
different cultures?

    Low                          Average                         High
--- 1 ----------- 2 ----------- 3 ----------- 4 ----------- 5 ---

**Comfort in the Language**
How comfortable are you in the language of the place
you are moving to?

    Not at all                   Somewhat                        Very
--- 1 ----------- 2 ----------- 3 ----------- 4 ----------- 5 ---

presented in this chapter. Based on your self-assessment, identify the strengths you can leverage, as well as where and how to begin improving the skills you need to build. Try some of the strategies I provided for building up resilience and cultural sensitivity.

Few are born to be ideal expatriates. You can't change your personality traits, but you can decide to make the most of what you have and develop what you don't have. In order to do that, accepting and 'owning' where you're coming from personality-wise is an important first step in determining your development goals and path to achieving them. Part of that development will happen without your noticing, as expat life itself will teach you some of the coping skills you need.

## CHECKLIST

- What aspects of your personality make it easier for you to embrace change? Which ones make it harder? What are the implications for what you need to focus on compensating for as you move?

- Would it help to get some deeper insight into your personality and its impact on your adaptability? If so, are there convenient ways to get that assessment done; for example, through your company?

- Do you consider yourself to be flexible and resilient? If yes, what is it about your personality and experiences that has made you adaptive? If not, what experiences could help you become more flexible and resilient?

- If you have moved before, how has it changed you? Do you expect this move to make you different and, if so, how?

4

**PRINCIPLE #4:**
YOUR PARTNER
MATTERS

Nancy had not expected the move with her family to be so much more challenging than the ones she had made on her own. Born and raised in Boston, she first moved abroad when she was in her mid-20s to work for an international NGO in Asia. The same NGO then took her to Africa and, finally, Europe. Despite the challenging locations, she didn't remember the moves themselves being difficult.

After she moved back to the US and married Chris, they talked about living abroad. Chris shared her taste for adventure. When their two daughters were still young, Chris got an offer from a venture capital firm in Stockholm, and they decided to go for it. They saw it as a chance to experience the European way of living. Nancy ran a small consulting business in Boston successfully and decided to keep running it from Sweden. They agreed up front that if things didn't work out, they would return to the US.

The first year in Stockholm was tough. Because of the time difference, Nancy's peak working times were afternoons and evenings, after the kids were in bed. She also had to travel to the US every few weeks to meet with her team and clients.

Despite all her efforts, the business did not thrive, and she had to close it down. That caused a lot of emotional and financial stress and had an impact on the rest of the family. Nancy tried to get a job in Stockholm, but she did not speak

Swedish, so her options were limited. When she suggested to Chris that they move back to the US, where she would have more career opportunities, he refused. She found herself trapped, unable to work and unable to leave. Unsurprisingly, their marriage suffered. In the end, they decided to separate. Nancy moved back to Boston with their girls, taking a job with a small biotech company. Chris quit his job and followed a few months later, so that he could be close to his daughters.

The struggles Nancy and Chris experienced are a good illustration of the impact of moving with a partner and potential relationship stresses associated with changes in roles and social isolation. How your partner fares during an international move and the quality of your relationship will have an impact on the overall success of the move. Studies over the last three decades have shown the spouse's adjustment to be a critical determinant of assignment completion, expatriate adjustment and successful expatriate performance, and a negative predictor of thoughts of withdrawal.[1]

Spouse/partner commitment to the move, starting with the initial decision, has been shown to be critical. 'Partner or spouse employment issues' was the second most-stated reason employees turned down an expatriate assignment, according to survey data from 2012.[2] The 2016 "Global Mobility Trends Survey" by Brookfield Global Relocation Services (BGRS) confirmed that finding, with concerns over spouse/partner careers and income featuring as the second most common reason for assignment refusal. Just over 80% of companies taking part in the survey indicated that spouse/partner employment was having an impact on their ability to attract qualified employees for international assignments.[3]

## THE COMPLEXITIES OF MOVING WITH A PARTNER

When you are the only one moving, decision-making is relatively straightforward. You call the shots and there are few, if any, compromises to be made. You only have to manage your own adjustment challenges, needs and expectations, and finances. Flexibility, freedom, possibilities, adventure and excitement are some of the words people associate with moving alone.

When you move with a partner, decisions need to be negotiated, different personalities and perspectives have to be taken into account, as well as potential differences in concepts of home and adjustment needs. There are, of course, real benefits to moving with a partner, including having an emotional support system and a relationship base from which to operate. One partner may be able to devote more time to building up your new local support system and navigate the process of settling the family, while the other focuses on performing well in the new position. At the same time, there are significant sources of complexity when you move with a partner.

- **Negotiated Decision-Making** – Most decisions will need to be negotiated, including: how to time the move so it works for both partners; choosing where to live; how to figure out transportation; who takes care of the new banking setup, and so on.
- **Different Concepts of Home** – Partners may have different concepts of home and this increases the challenge of creating a mutually satisfying home at the new location.
- **Different Personalities and Capabilities** – Different traits, abilities and skills also add complexity to the joint adaptation experience, especially when they make partners adjust at a different pace.
- **Different Degrees of Required Adjustment** – Someone who is familiar with the environment, the culture, the people, the way things work or who speaks the local language most likely will adjust more easily than someone who isn't. At the same time, this may make the 'local' partner feel responsible for the 'non-local' one's adjustment.

- **Different Perspectives of the Move** – Finally, partners often experience the move and adjustment process differently, which may cause friction in the relationship.

**Figure 4.1** presents an informal diagnostic tool for you and your partner to assess the complexity of your situation. Ideally, you will both answer the questions below and discuss them as you do that – or at the end.

## Figure 4.1: Complexity Diagnostic

### 1. Concept of Home
What is home for you and your partner? Make some notes in the table below. The degree of overlap or divergence in your concepts of home will give you an idea of the potential complexity in making the transition.

| Concept of Home | Place | Feeling | People | Everywhere | Nowhere |
|---|---|---|---|---|---|
| You | | | | | |
| Your partner | | | | | |

### 2. Personality Traits (Big Five)
Answer each question for you and your partner by marking yourself using **A** and your partner using **B** along the scales below. Where are the greatest divergences between you? These are areas of potential complexity that you will need to address early on.

**Openness**
How open are you to new experiences?

| Not at all | Somewhat | Average | Substantially | I love change |
|---|---|---|---|---|
| --- 1 --------- | 2 ---------- | 3 ----------- | 4 ----------- | 5 --- |

## Conscientiousness
How high is your ability and need for structure and organization?

| Low | | Average | | High |
|---|---|---|---|---|
| --- 1 | 2 | 3 | 4 | 5 --- |

## Extraversion
How extroverted/introverted are you?

| Introverted | | Mid-Range | | Extroverted |
|---|---|---|---|---|
| --- 1 | 2 | 3 | 4 | 5 --- |

## Agreeableness
How would you rate your tendency to be friendly, compassionate and cooperative?

| Low | | Average | | High |
|---|---|---|---|---|
| --- 1 | 2 | 3 | 4 | 5 --- |

## Neuroticism
How likely are you to experience negative emotions? The less often you do, the more emotionally stable you are.

| All the time | Often | Sometimes | Rarely | Never |
|---|---|---|---|---|
| --- 1 | 2 | 3 | 4 | 5 --- |

## 3. Other Personal Attributes
Answer each question for you and your partner by marking yourself using **A** and your partner using **B** along the scales below.

### Flexibility
How would you rate your ability to go with the flow?

| I need control | | | | Easy-going |
|---|---|---|---|---|
| --- 1 | 2 | 3 | 4 | 5 --- |

**Resilience**
How would you rate your ability to bounce back from adversity and stress?

| Low | | Average | | High |
|---|---|---|---|---|
| --- 1 | ---------- 2 | ---------- 3 | ---------- 4 | ---------- 5 --- |

**Cultural Sensitivity**
How would you rate your ability to function effectively in different cultures?

| Low | | Average | | High |
|---|---|---|---|---|
| --- 1 | ---------- 2 | ---------- 3 | ---------- 4 | ---------- 5 --- |

**Comfort in the Language**
How comfortable are you in the language of the place you are moving to?

| Not at all | | Somewhat | | Very |
|---|---|---|---|---|
| --- 1 | ---------- 2 | ---------- 3 | ---------- 4 | ---------- 5 --- |

**Risk-Taking**
Are you a risk taker?

| Never | Occasionally | Average | Often | Always |
|---|---|---|---|---|
| --- 1 | ---------- 2 | ---------- 3 | ---------- 4 | ---------- 5 --- |

**Degree of Required Adjustment**
How familiar are you with the new location?

| Not at all | | Somewhat | | Very |
|---|---|---|---|---|
| 1 | ---------- 2 | ---------- 3 | ---------- 4 | ---------- 5 -- |

**Perspectives of the Move**
To what extent do you expect your experience of the move and that of your partner to be similar?

| Not much | Some | Significantly | A lot | Identical |
|---|---|---|---|---|
| --- 1 | ---------- 2 | ---------- 3 | ---------- 4 | ---------- 5 --- |

## THE IMPACT OF DEEPER RELATIONSHIP STRESSES

While the complexities of making a move as a couple inevitably put the relationship under stress, their effect tends to be relatively manageable and short-lived. What really stresses the relationship is a set of subtler, deeper tensions. The solidity of your bond will determine how resilient your relationship will be through the relocation. The move can act as a catalyst, strengthening a strong foundation, or precipitating the collapse of a weak one. Key stressors for the relationship that are linked to a move include the following three factors: misalignment of motives, social isolation and changes in roles.

### 1. Misalignment of Motives

Susan met her partner, James, in Tokyo. She's American; he's British. When they met, he had been there for 10 years and she had just arrived the year before. He wanted to leave and she talked him into staying for another three years. This caused tension between them. When things went wrong, James quietly blamed Susan, and she, in turn, felt guilty.

"I loved him dearly and wanted him to be happy, but I needed this experience. It was my first time as an expat after growing up in the rural Midwest, and I needed to see it through for my own growth as a person. I was young and told him this in my own way. I wish I had the communication skills I have now, so that I could have expressed this to him in greater depth, and the listening skills to really hear him, too."

When partners don't share common goals, it can have a powerful impact on the relationship and the expatriate experience as a whole. The degree to which both partners are truly on board with the decision to move is a powerful predicator of success or failure. If one is more or less eager to move than the other, it can put the relationship under serious stress. When there is a recognized divergence, there is the potential to address it. But too often, it goes unnoticed until it's too late. Then, relationships can come under severe strain or even break up.

A move that is decided jointly and where both partners are committed to make it work has a different impact on the relationship than one that is considered a sacrifice by one of the partners. A 2005 survey showed that expat spouses who felt pressured to accept an international assignment had significantly poorer adjustment than those who felt involved and interested in the move from the beginning. Similarly, those who felt that the decision to relocate was shared between them and their spouses had a better adjustment track record.[4]

## 2. Social Isolation

Paula feels very strongly that the move to Austria put her marriage to the test. "I see us as a strong couple, but it has been very stressful. Back home in Brazil, it was easier because we were always around other people, family and friends. We didn't need to look into each other's eyes all the time. When there was a problem we talked and shared it and it went away. Here, we don't have that. It is the two of us all the time … what's good is very good, but also what's bad is very bad, because everything stays between us. Thankfully, we had a strong foundation as a couple before we moved."

Especially in the first few months of relocation, you spend a lot of time together as a couple. You have not yet built your social circle or support network. When the stresses of relocation create tension between you, there are no family or close friends around you to act as a buffer or a sounding board. In addition to that, relationship and marital troubles are often considered contagious and taboo to discuss, especially within expat circles, which further reduces your chances of getting support from your new community.

## 3. Changes in Roles

Kirsty and Carl, an American couple, met and married when they were both living in Paris. They both wanted to lead an expat life and live in many different places together.

However, neither of them was willing to give up their career, so they decided that they would move only when both had acceptable professional options. They identified locations that allowed them to have an equitable but flexible arrangement, where they could take turns pursuing their careers, but neither would take a back seat. When their children were young, Kirsty cut back on her work for a few years, especially since Carl's position involved extensive travel. She later got back on track when the boys were in kindergarten, while Carl reduced his workload. When they moved to Zurich for her job, he took a sabbatical during the first year, got the children settled and then started interviewing for jobs.

Solange and George have a different arrangement. While she was a successful marketing professional when they met, after they got married they agreed that his career would take priority through a series of moves. Solange manages their household, raises their two children and has veto power over all location decisions.

The distribution of roles within a couple – often linked to the priority given to their careers – can be disrupted by relocation; both the roles and the balance of power may shift and require readjustment. For example, while both partners may be pursuing their respective careers before a move, after the move, one of them may have to put their career on hold or give it up altogether. Not all couples anticipate or are prepared to cope with those new realities, which can have serious consequences, including the build-up of tension and resentment.

Use the informal diagnostic on the next page, together with your partner, to assess the existence of stressors in your relationship.

## Figure 4.2: Relationship Stressors Diagnostic

Answer each question for you and your partner by marking yourself using **A** and your partner using **B** along the scales below.

**Motives**
How eager were you to make this move?

| Opposed | Not so eager | Neutral | Somewhat eager | Excited |
|---|---|---|---|---|
| 1 | 2 | 3 | 4 | 5 |

**Degree of Social Isolation**
Do you have friends and/or family in the place you are moving to?

| None | A couple | A few | Decent network | Feels like home |
|---|---|---|---|---|
| 1 | 2 | 3 | 4 | 5 |

**Change in Roles**
How much do you anticipate your respective roles to change after relocation?

| No change | | Moderate change | | Significant change |
|---|---|---|---|---|
| 1 | 2 | 3 | 4 | 5 |

## NAVIGATING THE CAREER MINEFIELD

If and how much relationships come under stress due to changes in roles depends both on the specific role structure and on whether it has been agreed and accepted explicitly by the partners. Couples have different kinds of arrangements going into international moves, including one-partner and dual-career moves.

## One-Partner Career Moves

In this case, one partner's career always leads the moves, while the other partner follows. Accompanying partners may choose to stay at home or work, but with the understanding that they are not the ones leading the moves.

The rationale for this arrangement often is pragmatic. Emma and her husband, both American, have been living in Europe for more than 20 years. His job always initiated their moves. Emma admits, "Even though I don't like the sound of it, the choice was clear: I studied music, he studied business. He was always going to earn more than I did. It made no financial sense for me to lead the moves, so we made a pragmatic decision."

While it is most common for men and their careers to lead the moves (currently, only around 25% of expatriate assignees are women),[5] the trend is changing.

## Dual-Career Moves

In dual-career arrangements, partners agree that each will pursue their career in a roughly equal way through the moves. There are several variants of these arrangements. Partners may aim to pursue their careers at the same time, which implies that every move has to accommodate both careers. Or they may take turns leading the moves: one partner takes up a career-advancing position, while the other partner takes a temporary step to the side (for example, makes a lateral career move or goes on sabbatical for part or all of the move), with the expectation that they will shift gears again with the next opportunity.

## The Challenges of the Trailing Spouse

Whether a couple has a one-partner-career or a dual-career arrangement, the reality is that many couples end up with one of the partners not working or underemployed. These partners often are referred to as trailing spouses, a label that is somewhat controversial in the expat community because of the subordinate role it implies.[6] At the same time, it reflects the uncomfortable reality experienced by many expat partners. According to a 2008 survey by the Permits Foundation, while almost 90% of accompanying spouses were working before their partner's assignment, only 35% were employed during the assignment itself, even though three quarters of the non-working spouses wanted to be employed.[7] The trend seems to endure since BGRS' 2016 "Global Mobility Trends Survey" reports that 65% of the partners of the married/partnered expatriates were employed before the start of the assignment, and only 16% of those previously employed spouses were employed during the assignment.[8]

Spouses who are able to find rewarding work are more likely to report a positive impact on adjustment to the location and on family relationships than spouses who are not. However, since many international moves can cause the career of one of the partners to suffer, the 'trailing spouse syndrome' is often a key contributor to strained or even damaged couple relationships.

**Practical challenges**
The many role and career challenges inherent in expat moves can lead to profound changes in couple dynamics. Even if partners have agreed to pursue their careers simultaneously, both may not find equally career-advancing or fulfilling opportunities with every move. They may have to make tough choices, and one may have to compromise and end up dangerously financially dependent on the other – a situation I call 'the expat cage'.

Perhaps the most common problem is the inability of the expat spouse to secure a work permit. In some locations, the ('dependent') visas issued to accompanying partners or spouses limit the kind of contractual employment they can take up, sometimes even extending to volunteer work. Same-sex partners or spouses may face additional complications in countries where their partnerships, or even marriages, are not recognized, making them unable to receive residence and work permits, health insurance and other benefits. Oliver, British, and Giovanni, Italian, met in Milan, where Oliver was on assignment with a UK-based financial services firm. When Oliver was offered a position in Hong Kong by his employer, they decided to take it, even though they had found out that Giovanni would not be able to get a residence or work permit as his partner, since their partnership was not recognized by the authorities. While they thoroughly enjoyed their time in Hong Kong, Giovanni was there on a tourist visa the whole time and had to travel out of the country every three months to keep it. Since he was not allowed to work in Hong Kong, he decided to study for an online degree. When Oliver was offered a posting in Paris two years later, they went for it, so that they would both be able to pursue their careers.

Work permits are not, however, the only obstacle for accompanying partners trying to pursue their careers through successive relocations. They often need to rebuild their professional network from scratch in every new location. The type of work they do might not be available in the new location or may require knowledge of the local language. Their qualifications may not always be valid or accepted, and they may need to pursue further education. Some companies may be reluctant to hire someone who is bound to move again soon. Career support from their partner's employer is often minimal or non-existent, as many companies do not address spouse career issues (though that is changing).

All these obstacles make compromises inevitable. These are a heavy price to pay for today's expat partners, who increasingly are young, educated career professionals. The 2008 Permits Foundation survey, mentioned earlier, reported that 82% of spouses or partners of expatriates have a university degree.[9] Often, as we saw earlier, career-related concerns and dilemmas are the reason many dual career couples choose not to move or not to move together.[10]

Besides the practical challenges, expat partners often face substantial emotional challenges, including lack of connection and loneliness, loss of identity and dependence, especially financial.

## Loneliness and lack of connection

When one partner works while the other one stays at home, they function in different environments and have different experiences. Their daily life is structured differently and therefore the challenges they face are also different. A 2008 study found that the stress experienced during relocation differs substantially between partners. Expatriate employees are more stressed by relationship strains (coping with conflicting demands and expectations, dealing with their partner's disappointment linked to the move and the declining quality of the relationship), while their spouses are more stressed by the everyday difficulties of functioning in a foreign culture, isolation and lower self-esteem.[11]

The working partners generally arrive at the new location with defined roles and responsibilities and enter an established organizational support system. Integration comes easier through structured interaction. Even if the relocation involves working for a new employer, rather than transferring within the same company, the process is still relatively familiar. They are usually so busy adjusting to the demands of their new position that they do not have time to experience culture shock.

Their partners, on the other hand, are often thrown into new cultures without much preparation, support structure, or defined roles and responsibilities. The initial experience may be intimidating and stressful, as they have to handle the full range of logistics, from finding a home to opening bank accounts, creating a social circle and support network, building routines and, if there are children, making sure they are well settled. This is in addition to navigating their own adjustment process. Often, the working partner is unavailable for support.

A move can also be a lonely affair for accompanying partners. Having left their support networks behind, in the beginning, they spend a lot of time alone. They don't have an office (or school) to go to every day. They don't know many people. Their days are long. Their partner spends most of his day at work or is away on business trips. It's easy to feel isolated and lonely. Sometimes, these feelings turn into resentment. Too often, they can lead to grief, even depression.

Feelings of loneliness and isolation may be even more pronounced for males who are trailing spouses.[12] While it is often assumed that the issues faced by female and male trailing spouses are similar, there are, in fact, significant gender-specific differences in needs, challenges and the way each one adjusts. For instance, since trailing spouses are women by a large majority, male trailing spouses may find it hard to tap into their communities. They are often the 'odd man out' (pun intended) and have even fewer opportunities for social networking and creating connections, since most networks are built around the needs and socializing modes of female expat partners. As the numbers of female assignees increases, and male trailing spouses become more common, this will most likely change.[13]

## Loss of identity

When you have a couple in which both have similar educations and professional accomplishments, but only one takes the lead, it is hard not to imagine the potential for frustration, envy, resentment and other strains on the relationship. While one partner is fully immersed in their new job and concentrating on proving themselves, the other partner – who is equally educated and accomplished – sits at home, isolated and frustrated by the lack of professional opportunities, regretting having sacrificed their career. Going from a rewarding career with an established social system and support network to being a stay-at-home spouse and/or parent is a huge adjustment, in addition to the many challenges of building a life in a new country. Even if you have chosen not to work and/or even if the arrangement you have agreed on with your partner makes sense, financially or otherwise, as the trailing partner, you may still suffer from it. Many expat partners go through long periods of struggling to redefine their roles and create new identities for themselves.

Re-establishing credentials and recreating a professional network from scratch takes time. In the meantime, self-esteem suffers. Brigit, the Norwegian expat who moved to the US, felt the loss of identity very strongly. "Everything revolved around this university, but it was not my university. I felt like my whole identity was linked to my husband. I wanted my own area. I needed to find a purpose."

Emilia, a Hungarian expat who moved to the UK and then the US for her husband's career, had a similar experience. "Back in Budapest, we had equivalent university degrees and social status. We were earning equally. When we moved to the UK, I lost a lot of my power. He moved on, educationally and professionally, and I could no longer keep up." It is common for accompanying partners to experience resentment when their partner's career takes off at the expense of their own.

### Dependence, financial and other

Expat partners also often suffer from a loss of autonomy, particularly financial. Financial dependence not only affects their sense of identity and self-esteem, but it can also be a risk factor when things go wrong. Some expat partners become trapped in unhappy marriages, simply because they cannot afford to leave or because they worry about being able to assert their child custody rights in their country of residence. Or, if the working partner dies unexpectedly, the dependent spouse (and family) may face financial distress.

For many accompanying spouses, emotional dependence is also an issue. When you move away from your familiar surroundings and support system, your partner becomes your sole source of support – practical and especially emotional.

For some partners, this new-found neediness comes as a shock. They feel vulnerable. They also feel irritated or even resentful when the working partner, understandably preoccupied with work or physically absent, is unable to offer them the emotional support they need in those first days, weeks and months before they have set up their own support and social network.

This is not at all to say that it is going to be all bad. The non-working partner may be more involved in the community, build local contacts, get to learn the new language and have a much more enriching cultural experience than the working partner. Joanna, a Californian executive, describes how her writer husband's experience when they moved to Shanghai was very different from hers: "I work in an office where business is conducted in English and during the day it's no different than any other place I've lived. When I leave the office, I have difficulties with things like navigating the supermarket, because I do not speak the language, but I've always been adventurous and nothing really gets to me. Now, my husband, he's the one who's in the foreign country, not me. He's the one who gets to experience it every day."

But do not underestimate the potential damage that perceptions of sacrifice can do to the relationship. Tensions and build up of resentment can put enormous strain on relationships and may lead to hostility, even a breakup. In addition, on a personal level, all these feelings of loss, resentment and negativity can lead to anxiety, depression, or even substance abuse for the accompanying spouse.

There is, therefore, a real need for sufficient and appropriate support to make sure both partners make a successful transition both in the short, medium and long term. Investing the time and effort to set up such support structures is not a luxury, but a necessity for a successful relocation. Supporting your partner also brings real benefits to both and to your relationship. A study by Carnegie Mellon University found that people with supportive spouses are more likely to take on potentially rewarding challenges and, later, experience more personal growth, happiness, psychological wellbeing and better-functioning relationships. According to the lead author of the study, "Significant others can help you thrive through embracing life opportunities … or they can hinder your ability to thrive by making it less likely that you'll pursue opportunities for growth."[14]

The chapters that follow will show you how you can organize the necessary support for your partner at every phase of the move.

# CHECKLIST

- To what extent do you and your partner have similar concepts of home? If they are different, what are the implications for how you will create home together at your new location?

- To what extent are your personalities similar or different? What are the implications of differences in traits for the challenges you are likely to face throughout the move?

- To what extent have past experiences influenced how you and your partner deal with challenges during transitions? Are there things you can do to increase flexibility and resilience? What are some 'shock-absorbers' you can create to help during the adjustment process?

- Is the move likely to create significant changes in your roles? If so, what should you do to deal with the consequences?

- Is one of you hoping to find employment and/or continue developing their career at the new location? If so, what can be done to support that process?

5

**PRINCIPLE #5:**
YOUR CHILDREN
MATTER

*"When it comes to international relocation, most organizations deal with children as an afterthought. Factoring employees' children into the relocation equation is key to a successful assignment. Studies show that transferee children who have a difficult time adjusting to the assignment contribute to early returns and unsuccessful completion of international assignments, just as maladjusted spouses do."*

**Society for Human Resource Management,**
"Managing International Assignments"

Kate's son, Adam, was six years old when they moved to London from Washington, DC for her husband Jonathan's diplomatic assignment. Adam had difficulties adapting to his new life. Kate remembers: "He was having tantrums. He developed a pickiness with food that would not go away. He wasn't eating! Maybe he thought that if he got sick enough, they would send us back to the US."

This came as a surprise to his parents. "We thought Adam would be fine because he was an easy-going child, but we were wrong. He was easy-going in the US, but when we took him out of his familiar environment, suddenly he was not so relaxed."

Adam's troubles affected Kate's own adjustment to a great extent. "When he was not doing well, I was homesick, because I thought had we been at home, he would not have had those issues. I felt guilty for putting him through this." Eventually, Adam started feeling more comfortable in his new environment, and that had an impact on his taste for British food. Still, Kate remembers, "Some of the pickiness he developed in the UK has remained to this day."

Moving with children can be both a more complex and intense experience than moving as an individual or as a couple. While there are many positive aspects to moving with children (it can be a uniquely enriching experience for the whole family, and having children usually makes it easier for their parents to build social connections), a family move can also be demanding and stressful. Children are even less equipped than you are to withstand the challenges of an international move, and you are their primary source of support. Preparing children for a move, making decisions for them and making sure they settle in well are just some of the responsibilities you and your partner have as parents.

If your children are having a hard time adjusting, this will have an impact not only on the wellbeing of the whole family, but also on your performance and ability to contribute at work.

## IT'S DIFFERENT FOR CHILDREN

Moving and living abroad has many benefits for children. They learn to navigate different cultures and ways of life, become more resourceful, open-minded and tolerant, and increase their language and communication abilities, among others. In HSBC's 2016 "Expat Explorer Survey", expat parents report key advantages of raising their children abroad, including their children becoming open to new experiences and cultures (69%), learning new languages (59%) and becoming more well-rounded and confident (45%). In addition, nearly half of expat parents identified their children's wider, more diverse circle of friends as a benefit of expatriation.[1]

However, it is very important to keep in mind that children adjust differently to the experience of moving than adults do. They also have less control over the decisions about whether and where to move. As a result, they need additional and different kinds of support. Knowing where they're coming from and what influences their adjustment can help you as a parent to support them in the best possible way before, during and after a move.

Robbie and Angela moved with their parents from Cape Town to Berlin when they were four and nine years old, not speaking a word of German. Sylvia and Ben, their parents, put them in the local school and, within four months, not only were they fluent, but they also did a great job at imitating a Berlin accent.

It is conventional wisdom that children pick up new languages extremely fast, make new friends easily and are tremendously adaptable overall. There is some truth to that: when faced with the need to change, children often end up being remarkably resilient. Like Angela and Robbie, they are fast at picking up cultural cues and adjusting their behaviour accordingly, as well as learning new languages. However, being able to cope is not the same as liking it or adjusting to it easily. Why? Because fundamentally, children don't like change. They are creatures of habit. They also don't like uncertainty. Moves are the very essence of such change and uncertainty.

In addition, younger children don't choose to move, yet have to deal with the consequences and the dramatic change it brings to their lives. They are in a very different situation compared to their parents: they are not part of the decision-making. In fact, since children are usually not involved in major decisions related to a move, they may feel powerless, with little control over their lives. As they weren't involved in the decision, there often is a basic disconnect in how children and their parents approach a move. For parents, the focus is on moving forward (getting things organized, planning ahead, anticipating challenges), while for children it is on looking back at what they are leaving behind (their home, their friends, their routines). Their basic question is, 'why?' not 'whether' or 'when' or 'how'. They often start by fighting the move, disliking everything around them.[2]

As a result of all these factors, culture shock and the stages of adjustment are different, since children don't see the benefits of getting to know a new culture. Also, all the new experiences they stand to gain mean that they leave an equal number of elements behind: family, friends, school, favourite places, connections, rituals and routines. Instead of going through a honeymoon stage, like an adult would, they may be thrust immediately into a process of loss and grief as soon as the decision to move is made or even as soon as the possibility is raised.

Of course, not all children respond to the experience of moving in the same way. Reactions and processes of adjustment depend on intrinsic factors such as the age, stage of development of the child and their personality, as well as situational factors, such as the magnitude and timing of the move, and the parents' ability to maintain a sense of home. The particular way a child adjusts will also determine the kind of support it needs to make a smooth transition.

## Age and Stage of Development

When our family moved to Switzerland, our oldest son, who was ten at the time, had a hard time adjusting. He entered sixth grade in the Swiss system and was the new kid in a class that had been together since first grade. He did not speak Swiss German, while all his classmates did. He was homesick for Vienna. Unable to make sense of all that or verbalize it, he would throw temper tantrums and walk out the door every time we had an argument. By contrast, our eighteen-month-old son breezed through the transition, as if he had lived in Zurich all his life. He just absorbed everything around him, in wonder. While for our eldest Vienna was home, a few months into our move to Zurich, our youngest did not even remember ever living there.

Children of different ages experience moves differently. A key reason for that is a difference in how they perceive home.

An infant or any child under two years old may not be bothered much by a change in environment as long as their parents are there – because they are the child's home. For children who have not yet entered school (two to five years old), home is fundamentally about parents as well, but also about continuity in their very local, physical environment of the home, and specifically the details of their bedroom. Those elements are relatively easy to maintain through a move.

As children start elementary school (usually around six or seven years of age), and especially as they move into the teenage years, home becomes more centred around friends and social networks, as well as the broader physical environment beyond their home. In fact, their ability to learn how to navigate around their home is a source of pride and gives them a sense of independence and control, which are also crucial at that age. Moving, therefore, has a more significant emotional impact because it is equated with the loss of all these elements: familiar places, relationships and a support network, identity and a sense of belonging. Loss brings grief. In Chapter 2, I discussed briefly the stages a grieving person is likely to go through. Children are not always able to recognize or express that grief. In fact, they may sometimes feel ashamed or believe that they are not allowed to have *any* negative feelings, because this would indicate a lack of appreciation for all the exciting opportunities they are offered by living abroad.[3]

Children's losses and their reactions may not be easy to discern. Martha, Brazilian by origin, grew up in Japan, and then Brazil. Martha's family moved to the US when she was fifteen and initially she had a hard time adjusting. Her mother sensed that. When she asked her how she was feeling about her new life, Martha replied: "I have no struggles. I get to go to any school I choose, I live in one of the best countries in the world, I travel the world, my parents are home, and we live very well compared to other people." Although Martha was suffering, she did not feel that she had the right to complain about her situation. When her mother dug deeper into her daughter's feelings, she found shame and guilt, because her daughter was constantly comparing herself to other, less fortunate peers – especially from her country of origin.

While younger children tend to be more open to change and less affected by it, the older the child, the more resistant they are to the idea of moving. The longer a child has lived in the previous home, the deeper the roots that they have developed, and the more challenging it will be for them to move. On the other hand, parents can communicate much better with older children and explain the reasons for moving – the new culture and other elements – that can help with adjustment.

Moves hit teenagers the hardest, and I generally recommend against doing it, if possible. Teenagers have to cope with moves while in the midst of another big transition: puberty. Especially between the ages of 12 and 15, children go through a lot of physical and emotional changes. Their circle of friends is the most important source of support for them to cope with these changes. Their life and identity are built around their friends. Moving means losing that support, at least in the short term. As a result, teens have a harder time coping with the normal changes of adolescence, while also having to cope with the challenges and stresses of relocation. In some cases, if they have a hard time building a new social circle, this may have a broader impact on their ability to make friends and fit in with new social groups.[4] Finally, teens also typically develop a strong need for independence, a separate identity and control over their lives. A move threatens their ability to fulfil those needs.

Depending on their age and level of emotional develop-opment, children reveal the impact a move has on them in different ways. Often, they are not able to communicate how they feel, either because they do not know how to express it or because they don't want to disappoint their parents and impose additional stress on them. Parents may be too focused on why the move is so great for their children to listen to their concerns. Younger children may express their struggle through defiant behaviours, tantrums, or an exaggerated reluctance to take risks. Older children may go through changes in their sleeping and eating habits, moodiness or a tendency to isolate themselves. Eating difficulties, like Adam's from the beginning of this chapter (or even full-blown eating disorders), are not uncommon among children who experience the need to control *something* in their lives when they may feel too overwhelmed by the changes brought about by a move.

## Personality

As with adults, personality shapes how children adapt to a move. A 2010 study found that relocating is more challenging and has a longer-term effect on the wellbeing of children who exhibit particular personality traits, such as introversion or the tendency to be moody, nervous or anxious.[5] Moving makes it harder for them to maintain the close relationships that sustain them. Extroverted children, who tend to be more social and outgoing, may make friends easier and feel settled sooner than more introverted ones. Similarly, children whose personalities tend towards anxiety may see moves more negatively and struggle more with transitions.

As much as personality plays a role in how children experience transitions, sometimes they will surprise us. We may expect an introverted child to have a harder time adjusting than an extroverted sibling because the latter will be more comfortable reaching out and making friends. However, the introvert may also be much more comfortable being alone – an unavoidable reality in the first few weeks in a new place – while the extrovert may feel lost during that same time, without a crowd of friends around them.

It is, therefore, important to anticipate the impact of personality and try to compensate for it where possible. At the same time, it is important to keep an open mind and not let our assumptions create self-fulfilling prophecies.

## Assessing the Challenges, Part I: Age and Personality

Answer the questions below to get an idea of potential adjustment challenges and support needs for your children.

### Age and Stage of Development
At what age/stage of development is your child/each of your children? Feel free to add columns for additional children.

|  | Child 1 | Child 2 | Child 3 |
|---|---|---|---|
| **Baby/toddler** | | | |
| **<7 years old** | | | |
| **8-10 years old** | | | |
| **Pre-teen (10-12 years)** | | | |
| **Teenager (13-18 years)** | | | |

## Personality
Answer each question for each one of your children, using a different colour marker, along the scales below. I found the following two personality dimensions to be most relevant for children.

### Extraversion
How extroverted/introverted is your child?

| Introverted | | Mid-Range | | Extroverted |
|---|---|---|---|---|
| 1 | 2 | 3 | 4 | 5 |

### Emotional stability
Where on this scale would you place your child?

| Tends to have negative emotions | | | | Tends to see things positively |
|---|---|---|---|---|
| 1 | 2 | 3 | 4 | 5 |

There are important situational factors, such as the magnitude and timing of the move, the parents' attitude, as well as the ability to preserve home during a move. Parents have significant control over these factors, and this can have a big impact on how children experience the shift.

## The 'Magnitude' of the Move

The bigger the move – in terms of geography, cultural contrast or continuity disruption – the more challenging adjustment will be for your child.

### Geographical/time distance

Children, especially at a young age, experience distances as significantly greater than adults do, because distance makes it so much more difficult for them to keep in touch with their loved ones. If you are moving somewhere far from your current home, your child may not be able to communicate as regularly as before with family and friends, due to infrastructure, time difference or cost. This may leave them feeling isolated and homesick.

### Cultural and linguistic similarity

If the culture of your host country is very different from that of the origin country (think of a German family from Hamburg moving to Shanghai), your child may initially feel disoriented and confused. Add to that a new language that they don't speak (at least for the first few weeks), and they may feel unable to make sense of their environment and at a disadvantage in making new friends at school or in their neighbourhood.

### Continuity in schooling

Finally, the school environment can have a big impact on your child's ability to fit into their new home. Changing countries may bring significant changes in the schooling system, including curriculum, teaching style and methods, workload, assessment and school starting ages. But schooling is more than the specific educational system; language and culture are an integral part of the experience. The child's age and the projected length of stay in the new country also play a role here.

Younger children are more adaptable and more adept at learning languages and usually adjust to a local school and new language quickly. The older the children are, the more they may benefit from being taught, at least partly, in a 'home' language (or a language they are fluent in), for instance, by attending an international school or a national school in that language (for example, Swiss school in Singapore). For families who move to a different country every few years, consistency in the schooling system becomes more important, so putting children in local schools every time may not be beneficial for their adjustment, even though it may help them integrate faster in their neighbourhood.

## Assessing the Challenges, Part II: 'Magnitude' of the Move

What is the time difference between the place you are leaving and the place you are moving to?

| None | <3 hours | 4-6 hours | 7-9 hours | >9 hours |
|------|----------|-----------|-----------|----------|
| 1 | 2 | 3 | 4 | 5 |

How similar/dissimilar are the cultures of the two places?

| Very similar | Some similarities | No overlap | Some contrasts | Big contrasts |
|--------------|-------------------|------------|----------------|---------------|
| 1 | 2 | 3 | 4 | 5 |

How comfortable is your child in the language of the place you are moving to?

| Not at all | | Somewhat | | Very |
|---|---|---|---|---|
| --- 1 --------- | 2 ---------- | 3 ---------- | 4 ---------- | 5 --- |

How would you rate the degree of continuity in your child's schooling with respect to the following factors?

| | Educational system (structure, methods, curriculum) | | Language | |
|---|---|---|---|---|
| | Same/ similar | Different | Same/ partly same (bilingual) | Different |
| Child 1 | | | | |
| Child 2 | | | | |
| Child 3 | | | | |

## Timing of the Move

Timing refers to the time of year the move takes place, but also to the age of the child and their developmental stage when they relocate. Timing is also important with respect to where the child is in terms of their schooling. The right timing can be a key success factor in a move or it can make things much harder and prolong the adjustment period for your child – and for you.

What is the best time of year to move? Assuming that there is a choice, school systems and schedules, holidays and traditions, and the weather patterns of your destination play a role here. Moving in the middle of the school year can be disruptive, particularly for older children. Tina and Magnus, a Swedish diplomatic couple, moved every two to three years, often with very little warning. This lifestyle became more problematic once their son Sebastian started school. On their most recent posting, from Paris to Bangkok, they had to move him in the middle of second grade. "He cried all the time. He was not able to sleep alone. We took him to a therapist, but even that did not help, because even though he knew what was happening to him, he could not fully verbalize it." It took about a year for Sebastian to adjust and feel integrated in his new school.

Moving during Christmas or other big family holidays and having to spend them in a new country with different customs, where you don't know a soul yet, can make the whole experience much harder for everyone. Moving in the middle of winter, where the days are short, the skies are dark and you can't do much outdoors with the kids, can be challenging compared to a summer move.

What is the best age for children to move abroad? While there is no right answer to this, generally, the younger the child, the easier it is to move. We saw earlier that younger children tend to be more adaptable and open to change, while older ones tend to be more resistant to change.

Children also are likely to experience a move differently depending on when they move in terms of the stage in their schooling. Moving during a natural 'break' in schooling, for instance, at the beginning or the early grades of elementary school, is easier for a child to cope with than if you move them right before the last year of elementary or middle school. Moving during the last two years of secondary school is usually a bad idea. Considering the educational system at both origin and destination is key.

### Assessing the Challenges, Part III:
### Timing of the Move

(This is particularly relevant for parents with school-age children.)

What time of year are you moving?

☐ Beginning of school year

☐ End of school year/During summer holidays

☐ Mid-year

☐ During winter holidays

At which point in your child's schooling system are you moving?

☐ Natural 'break' between segments on both sides

☐ Natural 'break' at origin, but not destination

☐ Natural 'break' at destination, but not origin

☐ Last year of a segment

☐ After first year of a segment

☐ Mid-segment

## PARENTS AS ROLE MODELS

Your children take their cues from you, whether they are toddlers or teenagers. They notice how you approach the move and adjust their behaviour accordingly. If you see the move as an adventure, if you are motivated and energized to explore your new home, this will encourage them to do the same. If you show little or no interest or desire to adapt, it is highly likely that your children will mimic that. If you and your partner are aligned in your commitment, support each other and work hard to make the move a success, your children will feel reassured. If you are stressed and frustrated, your kids will sense that. If you are calm, patient and positive that you will overcome the challenges and settle in well, your children will follow suit.

## THE ABILITY TO PRESERVE HOME

Having a sense of home is particularly crucial for children and makes a huge difference in how they cope with transitions. We saw earlier that home means different things for children of different ages.

Connection to the nuclear family is an important element of home for most expat children. Compared to children who grow up in one place, children who go through international moves tend to be much more connected to their nuclear families. Because there is no extended family around, they tend to find a sense of home with their parents and siblings, and to rely on them for love, affirmation, role models, support and a safe space.[6]

For school-age children, having a sense of control over their immediate environment helps them create home. When Norbert, a German executive, and his wife announced to their eight-year-old daughter, Nina, that they were moving from their home in Hamburg to Warsaw, her reaction was, "No way. I'm not going to go, I have all my friends here. You can move. I'll stay here." When they told her, however, that she could paint the walls of her new room pink and bring all her Barbie dolls with her, she changed her mind. "She felt empowered to create her own space and that gave her a sense of home."

Friendships, connection and a sense of belonging are a crucial part of home for older children and teenagers. As part of developing their identity, they need to feel connected and part of a social group. Relocation disrupts their ability to satisfy those basic needs, as they have to rebuild their social and support network and find home with new people. When David and his wife Vanessa moved from Manhattan to Lausanne with their three children – four, seven, and ten years old at the time – they decided to put them all in local French schools to fully immerse them in the language, so that they would get the most of the one year they were going to spend in Switzerland. They overesti-mated the degree to which the last two summers of French camp had prepared their children for this. Their oldest son, Peter, suffered the most, thrust into an environment where, besides being expected to function at a very high level of French academically (the same as the other ten-year-old Swiss kids in his class), he also could not under-stand what was going on around him, since none of the kids, and very few of the teachers, spoke English. This was a very alienating and isolating experience, and Peter struggled through the fall of that year in Lausanne. David remembers those first few months of the school year: "Peter does not complain and is generally stoic about virtually everything. When we moved to Lausanne, he was right in the middle of reading the *Harry Potter* series. So, every morning, in the car on our way to school, he would read one of those books, and he would take it with him when he left the car. I came to realize that on the breaks between classes, he would go and sit with his back up against the wall and he'd read that book, while all the other kids went out and played. This was his way of coping with the fact that he did not know any other children (they all had known each other since first grade) and could not really communicate with them due to his insufficient knowledge of French. That fall was a very difficult time, but after the first few months, the language began to kick in, and Peter began not only to understand what was being said at school, but also was able to make himself understood. That process was largely invisible to us until one day when I drove him to school and we arrived and he put the book down on the dashboard and got out of the car. I called to him, "Wait a minute, don't you want your book?" and he said, "No." For me, that signified the moment when he felt comfortable enough and connected enough in his new environment, with his new friends, that he did not need to go to another place."

The loss of family and friends is one of the biggest sources of stress for children going through relocation. Being able to stay connected with the loved ones they leave behind provides a sense of continuity and home.

Rituals and routines create a sense of continuity between the different chapters in children's lives and thus help them adjust. They reinforce family identity, since they are part of its common history. Every family has its own rituals.

## Assessing the Ability to Preserve Home

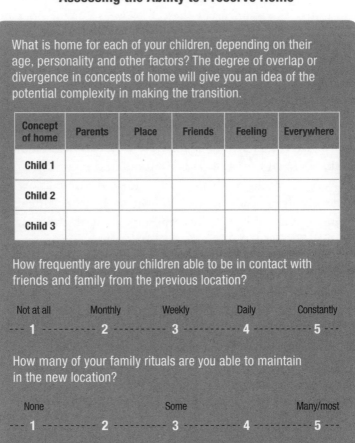

What is home for each of your children, depending on their age, personality and other factors? The degree of overlap or divergence in concepts of home will give you an idea of the potential complexity in making the transition.

| Concept of home | Parents | Place | Friends | Feeling | Everywhere |
|---|---|---|---|---|---|
| Child 1 | | | | | |
| Child 2 | | | | | |
| Child 3 | | | | | |

How frequently are your children able to be in contact with friends and family from the previous location?

| Not at all | Monthly | Weekly | Daily | Constantly |
|---|---|---|---|---|
| --- 1 | ----------- 2 | ----------- 3 | ----------- 4 | ----------- 5 --- |

How many of your family rituals are you able to maintain in the new location?

| None | | Some | | Many/most |
|---|---|---|---|---|
| --- 1 | ----------- 2 | ----------- 3 | ----------- 4 | ----------- 5 --- |

Living abroad is likely to create many exciting opportunities and bring unique benefits to your children. While children generally adapt well and eventually settle in fully in their new environments, moving can be a challenging time for them. Supporting your children before, during and after an international move to ensure that they make a smooth transition is not just your responsibility as a parent; it is also a precondition for the wellbeing of the whole family. That's why it is important that you invest the time and effort to make sure your children have the support they need for every phase of a move. The rest of the book will show you how you and your partner can organize and mobilize that support.

## CHECKLIST

- What are the biggest transition challenges your child or children are likely to face given their age(s) and stage(s) of development?

- Is your child (or some of your children) likely to struggle more with the move because of personality traits? If so, are there specific things you can do that would help?

- Overall, how 'big' is the move for your child(ren)? Are they likely to struggle to stay connected with friends because of distance and/or time differences? If so, are there ways you can compensate?

- If you have some flexibility in terms of when the child(ren) would move, what would be the best timing? What can you do during the time before the move to stay connected?

- What can you do to help your child(ren) preserve, to the greatest extent possible, a sense of home through the move?

# PART II

# FROM PRINCIPLES
# TO ACTION

You have established your intention for the move. You have clarified your goals, both immediate and longer term, and you've figured out how the move fits into the big picture of your life. You are also aware of the basic principles that should guide your approach towards making an international move. You have reflected on what home is for you and what you need to feel at home. You have a rough picture in your mind of the stages you are likely to go through in your adjustment process. You have assessed your personal attributes and understand how they could affect your adaptation. Finally, if you are moving with your partner or family, you are focusing on their needs, desires and expectations and preparing to provide them with the support they need to thrive through this transition.

Armed with that knowledge and awareness, it's time for action. So, we now will focus on concrete advice and tools to tackle each phase of the relocation – deciding, preparing, moving and settling in – in order to make it successful for you and for your family. The four chapters that follow, one for each phase of the move, will show you the areas you need to address and the specific steps you need to take to achieve success. Each chapter points out common traps to avoid and key strategies for making solid, informed decisions, thoroughly planning and preparing the ground, making a good move and settling well into your new home.

If you are not at the very beginning of the process, just start reading where relevant and go back later to read the rest of the chapters.

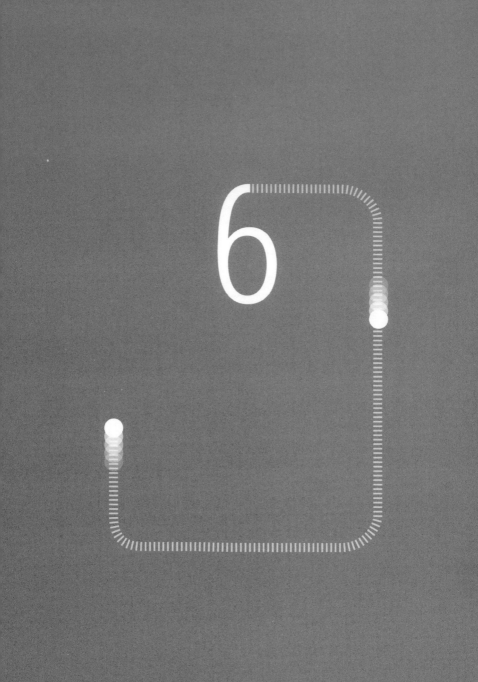

# 6

# DECIDING

*"Truly successful decision-making relies on a balance between deliberate and instinctive thinking."*

**Malcolm Gladwell**

Too many people decide to relocate without thinking through the implications of the relocation for themselves, their partners and their family. In my years of research on how people make moves, I have often seen people jump head first into what they consider to be an adventure, with serious consequences.

This was the case for Celine and Christophe. Originally from Montreal, Celine met Christophe, a native of Lyon in France, while they were students in Paris. They fell in love, decided to stay there, got married and had two children. Celine worked in marketing for a large French cosmetics company. When the children were sick and could not go to day care, Christophe's mother would take the train up from Lyon and stay with them, so neither he nor Celine had to miss work.

Christophe worked as a finance manager for an American multinational. When their children were six and eight years old, still in the early stages of elementary school, he was offered a promotion and a position at the company's Geneva branch. He was given two weeks to decide.

Christophe was thrilled and ready to go. He had been discussing the possibility of an expat assignment with his manager. It felt like a perfect opportunity for him professionally and a wonderful chance for the family to experience a different culture. He was confident that they could make it work.

Celine was less enthusiastic. Her company had just put her through leadership training to prepare her for a managerial position. She was hesitant to move just as she was starting to advance professionally. Still, she assumed that with her qualifications and work experience, it would be easy for her to get a new job. She had acquired French/EU citizenship from her marriage to Christophe, which meant that she would have no problems obtaining a residence permit and would be legally allowed to work in Switzerland.

Christophe took a quick trip to Geneva to visit the company offices and spent a few hours with a relocation consultant looking at housing. They accepted the offer, and Christophe got ready to go right away. They planned to move the family over the summer vacation, which was just three months away.

They had heard that Swiss public schools were very high quality and thought it would be a great way for their children to integrate into their neighbourhood and make local friends. Sometime in June, while they were finalizing preparations to move, they were informed that their six-year-old daughter, who was just about to start first grade in Paris, did not make the cut-off for first grade in the Swiss system and would have to stay an extra year in kindergarten.

It was only after they had moved that they discovered that Swiss public schools close for two hours during lunch and that children are expected to go home to eat every day. There was a lunch service available in their district, but it was expensive and they had already missed the deadline for registering for the semester. Celine had thought that she would get the kids settled at school for the first few weeks and then immediately move ahead with her job search (she had already gotten in touch with a couple of head-hunters before leaving Paris). Instead, she found herself needing to pick up her children and make lunch every day of the week. The school schedule made it impossible for her not only to look for a job, but also to actually work, since she always had to be home for lunch. She grew increasingly frustrated.

Meanwhile, Christophe hit the ground running in his new position. He and Celine had not discussed the details of his new role, and it came as a surprise to her that he was gone most of the week – either because he had late meetings at the office or was travelling – and was back home only on weekends. They had not had time to look into childcare options before the move, so Celine ended up having to set up their new home and get the family settled alone, in a new country where she knew no one and was unable to work. She became resentful and tensions at home mounted.

The experience of Celine and Christophe illustrates the dangers of rushing the decision to make an international move. Often, candidates are given tight deadlines for deciding whether to accept an international assignment. If this is their first expat move, they may have limited or no experience with international relocations and not know what to expect. To further complicate matters, the motives for the move differ between partners or spouses. The move may be a really good deal for one partner – Christophe's promotion is a good example – but not for the other – Celine having to give up her position while she was on her way up, and then finding that her ability to work right away in Switzerland was much more limited than she expected.

## COMMON MISTAKES

Many factors conspire to compress and complicate the decision-making process. When international moves are not thought through, there is the risk of falling into common traps that contribute to unnecessary strains and even failure of the assignment.

1. **Having unrealistic expectations**. Insufficient knowledge of the basics of the destination (e.g., the details of daily life) before making a decision can lead to unrealistic expectations of the impact of the move. Celine and Christophe had divergent expectations on who would take care of the move: he had been counting on her to manage the process of getting the family settled, while she had been counting on him to be around the first few weeks to help with part of that process. When that did not happen, he felt frustrated and she felt abandoned.

2. **Ignoring misaligned motives**. The move is likely to have different consequences for those involved in it. The result can be one partner strongly advocating for the move and the other suppressing their doubts and deciding to go along, only to experience regret or even anger later on. When one partner feels like they did not have a say in the decision, they are more likely to become resentful or resistant to adjusting. This has implications not just for the overall success of the assignment, but also for the couple's relationship. Given that partner dissatisfaction is the biggest reason why expat assignments fail, it's essential to make sure that both partners are fully on board with the decision and committed to making the move a success. Had Celine realized that she would have to put her career on hold for a while, she might have decided this was the wrong time for a move or gone forward with her eyes open. Instead, she felt like she had sacrificed her professional future for her husband's. This took a toll on their marriage and affected the whole family.

3. **Not thinking about broader implications**. Even when partners make a joint decision, it can still happen that they don't take time to think through and discuss the implications of the move for all family members, and how they will address them as a family. Here, too, the result can be misaligned expectations and unpleasant surprises later on.

Christophe and Celine's daughter being held back at school made the process of moving, which was already challenging, feel like a punishment, and undermined her confidence.

Being aware of these common pitfalls is the first step in designing a solid approach to deciding on a move. Still, making some early mistakes does not doom you to failure. As time passed and they started to settle down in their new home, Celine and Christophe found ways to work around their initial constraints. They met other parents from the school and found out that there were lunch shifts where parents took turns feeding lunch to a group of children. But it took almost a year before they had hired an au pair to take care of the kids in the afternoons and Celine was able to start a new position at a luxury goods company. The time frame for that would have been significantly shorter had they thought through the implications more thoroughly when they were making the decision.

## HOW TO DECIDE ON A MOVE

Given that you understand the importance of (1) making an informed decision, based on realistic expectations, and (2) ensuring that all stakeholders are on board with that decision and aligned in their expectations, the next step is to use a rigorous, structured process to make the critical decisions in the right ways. The six steps presented below will guide you through this process. You may not have a lot of time to go through all six steps. You may have to make a decision within a short time frame and with limited information. Even if you only have a weekend to decide, however, the steps that follow are still valuable because they can help you structure your approach and use your limited time productively to think through your decision.

## Step 1. Frame the Decision

Expat moves are life-changing events and not to be entered into lightly. So, to the greatest extent possible, frame your decision as a real choice. Ask yourself whether you really want the assignment. Don't assume you should go for it just because it's exciting. Stop. Consider. Will you go or will you stay? As you think this through, start with the 'why'. If you choose to go, what's your reason for going? Then focus on the pros and cons of making the move. For example, will the move open up new career options? Are there significant financial advantages to moving? Is the distance likely to make it harder for you to take care of your ageing parents? Look at the big picture and think about how this move fits into your long-term plans and goals – professional/career, personal development and family.

If you are making this decision to move jointly with your partner, explore *their* 'why' and how the move would fit with their medium- and long-term goals. Is this decision compatible with your partner's career plans and aspirations? What is their motivation for the move? If applicable, extend this thinking to every other member of the family.

## Step 2. Identify the Key Uncertainties

Next, identify what you do not know about the different aspects of the move and its impact on different areas of your life. What are the key uncertainties and their potential impacts? Look at the table opposite and circle the questions that are most important to you and, if applicable, to your partner. Then take the time to discuss them.

As you engage in discussions, don't forget to talk about your time horizon. How long are you planning or expecting to stay? What if this assignment is extended or you are offered a new one in a different location? Is this a one-time thing or an expat lifestyle choice, and what are the implications of such a choice for everyone involved? For instance, if your spouse plans to take a temporary career break or leave of absence from her work to follow you abroad, especially if her career is not portable, a short-term expat assignment would work fine. However, a longer-term assignment or series of assignments is something the two of you will need to plan for differently.

Also, even if it is far into the future, discuss your long-term plans for returning home. *Are* you planning to return?

## Table 6.1: Key Uncertainties by Area

| | Key Uncertainties | |
|---|---|---|
| | You | Your Partner |
| Work/Career | Will the corporate culture be similar to what I am used to? What challenges am I going to face doing business in a different culture? | Will I get a work permit? Will I be able to get a job? Will my skills and qualifications be valued in the new job market? |
| Personal | Will I feel safe in the new location? | Will I feel homesick? |
| Family | Will my partner be happy in the new location? Will the frequent travel required by my new position affect my relationship with my children? | Should my children go to an international or local school? Will we be able to maintain family traditions? |
| Friends and social life | Will I be able to build a social network in the new country even though I don't speak the language? | What are natural places for me to meet new people? |
| Financial situation | Will my salary be able to cover my/our needs in the new location? | Will I be able to be financially independent? |
| Physical environment, including climate | Will my body be able to cope with the heavy winter? | Are there parts of the city where expat families prefer to live? |

When? While it is often not possible to anticipate future developments in all these areas, it is important to at least discuss intentions and contingency plans. All this preparation, especially reflecting on your long-term goals and plans (or your respective plans if you're moving with a partner), will also help you be better prepared to decide when the next relocation opportunity comes.

## Step 3. Assess the 'Magnitude' of the Move

The greater the contrast between geographies, languages, customs, values and habits, the more effort it takes to adjust and the more skills you need to bring to the table.[1] To evaluate the magnitude of the move, start by researching the basics of your destination in order to get a good picture of what your daily life will look like. As you do this, you also should gather information that will help you reduce the key uncertainties you identified in step 2 of the process. Armed with more information, you can deepen your understanding of the consequences for you and others.

Use the information you gather to assess the magnitude of the move (the difference from your home or previous location) and how that will affect each family member. There are several dimensions of move magnitude, including geographical distance, cultural distance and distance from home. It is important to understand them and the impact they have, especially given family members' potentially different concepts of home.

### Geographical distance

How big is the move in terms of pure geographical distance from where you are now? If you are moving a substantial distance, how will that, including differences in time zones, affect your ability to stay connected with people you are leaving behind? How will your children react to the distance from friends and family or a reduced ability to communicate?

What about the climate of the new place? If you come from a temperate climate, harsh winters may be a serious shock to your system and be a cause of irritation or even depression. Also, consider whether you or anyone in the family has medical conditions that could be exacerbated by climate conditions in the new location. Ajay, an economics professor from Delhi, turned down an attractive offer to teach at a business school in Chicago and decided to take a job with a less prestigious school in Singapore instead, because the latter would allow him to be closer to his parents and extended family. Proximity to family is an essential part of home for him. Unfortunately, he did not anticipate that the overwhelming humidity of the climate in Singapore would cause him serious health problems. After two years of struggling and trying to make it work, he had to give up and move back to India.

### Cultural distance

Evaluate the degree to which you will be able to feel comfortable and at home there. How similar or different is the culture at the new location from your home culture? Will you have to learn a new language, and how challenging do you expect that to be? How expat-friendly is the new location? Is the infrastructure accessible even to those who don't speak the language? Is the society welcoming to foreigners? Is there a significant expat population? Are locals accustomed to dealing with foreigners?

The answers to all these questions will give you an idea of what will affect your ability to adjust and feel at home. Keep in mind that often the places where you think you will have the least difficulty adjusting are the ones that challenge you the most.

### Distance from 'home'

Finally, look at your destination through the lens of your concept of home (and the concepts held by your family members).

How challenging will it be to create home for you and your family at the new location? Use the table below to help you evaluate. Start by identifying the concept of home that is most important to you – place, feeling or people – and then look at the corresponding questions. Do this for every member of your family. What are the implications for the challenges you are likely to face, and what can you do to mitigate them?

## Table 6.2: How to Create Home?

| Concept of Home | Assessment Questions |
|---|---|
| **Place**<br><br>Assess how you connect to the physical environment of your destination. Focus on what works. | Do you feel connected to the landscape, e.g., you love being close to the water, but what if you need to move to a landlocked town?<br><br>If you don't feel naturally at home, are there elements that you relate to or that remind you of your physical home – that you can build on, e.g., if you love living in the countryside, but have to move to a city, can you find a place on the outskirts where you could be closer to nature? |
| **Feeling**<br><br>Assess how likely you are to feel comfortable in the new culture. | Do the values and beliefs of the new culture resonate with your values?<br><br>Do you fit in as a personality?<br><br>Are you comfortable in the language?<br><br>Even if you speak the language or are familiar with the culture, don't assume that you will fit in right away. |
| **People**<br><br>Assess the extent to which you will be able to maintain and build your network. | How easy will it be to meet new people and make friends? Will there be opportunities for socializing with colleagues, neighbours and other expats?<br><br>Is language a barrier to building a social circle?<br><br>Does your destination offer the infrastructure to maintain regular contact with friends and family back home?<br><br>If not, how easy will it be to set it up?<br><br>Is the time difference a limiting factor in maintaining those contacts? |

## Step 4. Understand the Assignment

It is important that you and your partner are aware of the specifics of the assignment, including the terms of the offer: role and expectations, including average weekly/monthly travel requirements, expected duration, terms of the offer (contractual obligations, expat package provisions, benefits). Ideally, both of you should be informed and involved in the contract negotiations, especially in selecting benefits (if applicable) and requesting additional support for the non-working partner or the family. Celine was not aware, for example, that Christophe would effectively be gone during their first few months in Geneva. Had they discussed this, they could have organized support for Celine (for instance, have his mother join them) for that period.

Thoroughly discuss the implications of the assignment for the different areas of your lives and how these fit with both of your medium- and long-term plans. Aligning expectations and anticipating challenges is crucial in making an informed joint decision. Without that, it's easy for one partner to end up feeling disempowered, disadvantaged or resentful. Both partners have to have their own, ideally equally strong motivations for making the move.

Assess first how the move will affect you personally. What will be the impact on your professional life, including your future career? What will be the impact on your personal life – social life, friendships, intimate relationships? How will the relocation affect your connection with your family? How will it affect your health and wellbeing, including pre-existing health conditions, and your ability to sleep enough, exercise regularly and engage in other activities that are important to your physical and emotional wellbeing?

If you are moving with a partner, they should answer the same questions – and you should discuss the implications. It's especially important to anticipate and discuss the impact of changes in roles and family dynamics as a result of moving.

How does each of you see the shift and new role distribution? Are you both comfortable with it? Be explicit here – it could make or break your move.

If you are a dual-career family and plan to both work in the new location, discuss your partner's career goals, options and constraints in the destination. What does your partner need to make this move work for them? Find out, before deciding if possible, whether your partner will be legally allowed to work in the new location and what the legal framework and requirements are for doing that (work permit).

Beyond the legal requirements, consider the practical and financial feasibility of working. Is there a language barrier? Do you anticipate issues with credential recognition and/or professional certification? If there are children, are there realistic childcare options to allow both partners to work outside the home?

All this will help you anticipate the kinds of resources you will need to secure as part of your contract or using your own means. Make a list of all those resources and be proactive in asking your employer for the support you need – for your partner and your children.

If only one of you will work, be clear about whether this a longer-term arrangement or whether you are planning to take turns pursuing your respective careers over time. Be explicit about your agreement – whatever that is – and align expectations.

Also, keep in mind that you will have to revisit and potentially renegotiate some of those agreements and understandings with every move. Always go back, realign expectations and reconfirm agreement on key points.

Use the table opposite to answer key questions, lay out the plusses and minuses for yourself and your partner and list resources that will help you cope better.

## Table 6.3: Assessment of Implications and Resources Needed

| | Implications/Pros & Cons | | Resources needed |
|---|---|---|---|
| | Self | Partner | |
| **Impact on professional life**<br>Career goals<br>Options<br>Constraints (e.g., legal requirements, credentialing, language barrier, childcare availability)<br>Long term career plans | | | |
| **Impact on personal life**<br>Ability to maintain existing friendships and intimate relationships<br>Ability to create new friendships and intimate relationships | | | |
| **Impact on contact with family** | | | |
| **Impact on health and wellbeing**<br>Ability to sleep, exercise, engage in hobbies | | | |
| **Other doubts, concerns, fears** | | | |
| **Will there be a change in family dynamics and how will it affect you?** | | | |

## Step 5. Think Through the Implications for Other Family Members

Before making a decision, discuss with your partner, and potentially with older children, how relocation will affect your children and other members of your family. For your children, answer the following questions:

- Given your children's age(s) and stage(s) of development, as well as cultural and geographical distance, and the timing of the move, how disruptive is it likely to be for them?
- How easy do you expect it will be for your child to adjust to the new location, given their personality? Will you be able to provide them with appropriate support? What are the biggest losses they are likely to experience (family, friends, routines)?
- Does your child need special care (for example, due to a medical condition, physical disability or learning difficulty) and will you be able to provide that at the new location?
- What are the schooling options in the new location? Will your child be able to continue their schooling in the same language as before? How affordable are the different alternatives? Exploring educational options *before* deciding to move is crucial.[2]
- How will the timing of the move affect their schooling experience and do you have any room to manoeuvre? If you cannot avoid moving mid-year, can your child at least continue in the same type of school system and language to make the adjustment a little smoother?
- How feasible will it be for them to maintain contact with their friends and family back home? How much support will they need from you to help them develop a new circle of friends?
- To what extent will their daily lives and routines be disrupted by relocation? While it is unavoidable that disruption will happen, will they be able to maintain at least

some of their routines or pursue favourite activities in the new location? For example, if your children are avid football players, will you be able to enrol them in a decent football program in the new location?

Use the following table to evaluate the implications for your children and assess the resources you will need to help them with adjustment.

### Table 6.4: Assessment of Implications and Resources Needed for Your Children

| | Implications/ Pros & Cons | Resources needed |
|---|---|---|
| Impact of age and developmental stage on adjustment | | |
| Impact of personality on adjustment | | |
| Special care requirements | | |
| Schooling<br>Continuity<br>Options available, including timing, affordability and other factors | | |
| Ability to maintain contact with loved ones back home | | |
| Ability to make new friends | | |
| Disruption of daily life<br>Ability to engage in favourite extracurricular activities<br>Ability to pursue routines and rituals | | |

In your current home, you most likely have a network of extended family, friends, other parents or colleagues to support you and your family. An international move disrupts that support system and it helps if you can anticipate what your needs will be. For instance, if you have children and both you and your partner plan to work in the new location, it is important to consider childcare availability and affordability.

Finally, how will moving affect your ability to fulfil your obligations concerning your extended family? Will you be able to stay in touch regularly and how? If you are taking care of aging family members – or anticipate having to take care of them in the near future – how will moving affect your ability to do that? Are there alternatives you can resort to?

## Step 6. Determine Whether Everyone Really is on Board

Having framed the decision, assessed the magnitude of the move, and evaluated the consequences, the final step is to see if you and your partner (and potentially your children) are on board for the move. This means making sure that you both feel empowered to say 'yes' or 'no'. A 'yes' would mean that you are fully committed to the decision and to making the relocation a success.

Also, depending on your child's age and level of maturity, consider whether it makes sense to involve them in discussions around the decision. There are pros and cons to involving them, but ultimately, you are the best judge of what is right for your family. If you decide not to involve them in the decision, then make sure you tell them as early as possible after the decision is made. The older they are, the sooner they should know, as they will need time to process the decision and adjust to the idea of moving. Give them that time. Also, children are very perceptive and usually sense when something is occupying you. Telling them early is important to avoid them guessing that there is something going on or, worse, finding out by accident.

Pick an appropriate time and a comfortable setting for telling them. Choose a time that gives them a chance to absorb the news. Telling them before they leave for school on Monday morning is probably not a good idea. Explain the reasons for the move. Even if the children were not involved in the actual decision, it is crucial that they understand how you came to this conclusion, why you think it makes sense, and what you are going to do to minimize disruption and sustain connection. Set aside enough time for them to express their feelings and thoughts and to ask questions. Try to find out and answer as many of their concerns as you can, to avoid them getting wrong ideas or worrying unnecessarily. Be honest and open about your own feelings. It is important to be able to give your children an initial idea of what to expect and a lot of reassurance. It also helps immensely to give them reasons to feel positive about the possibilities and to come on board with the decision. Maybe it is proximity to an old friend of theirs, or a new activity that they can pursue in the new place or trips you can take together to explore the new country.

Five years into their Geneva assignment, Christophe was approached by a head-hunter about a very attractive opportunity back in Paris. He was intrigued by the position and at the same time felt that it was time for their family to return home. Again, Celine saw things differently. It had taken her a while to get settled, but she was finally thriving professionally. The children were feeling at home in Geneva, had their routines and circle of friends and, besides, they were now eleven and thirteen. Celine was well aware that moving during the teenage years could be very disruptive. After a lot of back and forth, they decided that, for the time being, she would stay in Geneva with the children and that, if Christophe got the position, he would commute to Paris, at least for the first two years. Things might have been different if they had discussed their expectations with respect to being expats and returning home to France *before* that first move.

Making a solid, informed decision, where all stakeholders are aligned and on board is key to the success of your move and sets the stage for the phases that follow. Do your best not to rush the decision. And, once you've made it, own it. Commit to it. If you have decided to go, do your absolute best to make the most of it. The next chapters will show you how.

## CHECKLIST

- Have you framed the decision as a real choice? Are you prepared for 'no' to be the outcome? If you say 'yes', will you feel fully committed to making the move a success?

- Have you identified the uncertainties that would have the biggest impact on the success of your move? Are there ways you can gather more information to reduce uncertainty?

- How 'big' is the move in terms of geographical distance, cultural distance and ability to create home in satisfying ways? Are you really prepared to make a move of this magnitude?

- What will the assignment demand of the sponsored partner in terms of time, travel and other expectations? What is the implication for the other partner? Are you prepared to deal with these implications and/or are there ways to mitigate them?

- How will your children be affected by the move? What challenges are they likely to face? Are there ways you can reduce these challenges or support them in dealing with them?

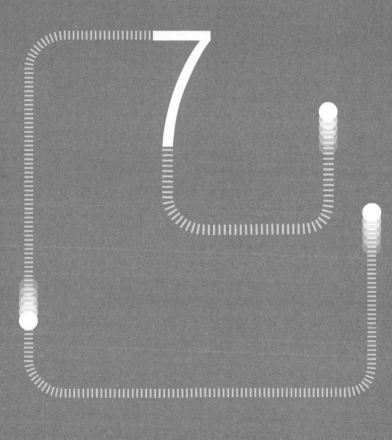

# 7

# PREPARING

*"Cross-cultural living can be a wonderful experience in countless ways, but it is far better when it begins with clear thinking and good planning rather than with naive visions of a romantic adventure."*

**David C. Pollock and Ruth E. Van Reken,**
*Third Culture Kids: Growing Up Among Worlds*

Lack of thorough preparation is a common source of difficulty in expat moves. Often, because of pressure to decide and move fast, assignees and their families do not have much time to prepare, in practical or emotional terms, for the big changes ahead. Without adequate planning, however, assignees may take longer to get up to speed at work, and also face challenges on the home and family front. Job and home frustrations can set the assignment up to fail.

Preparation for an international move means anticipating potential challenges and identifying the necessary resources to address them early on. Preparation is not just about handling the logistics. It is also about getting into the right mind-set.

Sabine and Alex had been married for ten years and had seven-year-old twin sons when they began their expat journey. They were living and working in Hamburg, he as a management consultant and she in human resources, when Sabine got an offer from her employer to relocate to Singapore. Their sons were still in elementary school, so they thought this was as good an opportunity as any to have an 'Asian adventure'. They spent a few weeks weighing the pros and cons for their careers and the family and decided to accept the offer. Alex would take a break from consulting and help the family get settled in Singapore, so that Sabine could focus on her new position and then, after a year, they would hire an au pair and he would get a job. With a six-month window to choose when to move, they decided that the family would go together at the end of June, just before summer vacation.

Before saying yes to the relocation, Sabine and Alex sat down and made a plan for their move, focusing on a few key priorities: finding schooling for their boys, securing adequate housing and making sure that Alex would be able to continue working in his field in Singapore. Fortunately, help in finding adequate schooling and housing was part of the standard relocation package. In addition, Sabine's employer provided three two-hour sessions of cross-cultural training for the whole family to help them get ready. Spouse professional support was not included in the package, but Sabine decided it was important to ask for that and managed to negotiate specialized career support for Alex into her contract.

The couple sat down with their sons and told them that the family was going on an adventure. They showed them pictures of the Singapore Zoo, the Gardens by the Bay sound and light show, and Universal Studios, and they talked to them about going on a night safari and swimming with dolphins.

They planned a short trip to Singapore, leaving the boys with Sabine's mother in Germany, to look at prospective houses, visit schools and get a feel for the city. Sabine's company put them in touch with a local relocation agent. Before leaving, they detailed their expectations for the ideal house and neighbourhood and asked to look at the German school there. They did some additional research, looking at expat forums and websites on life in Singapore, which helped them narrow down their search to a few neighbourhoods where a lot of expats lived and that were close to the school. While the boys were already learning English at school in Germany, the thinking was that enrolling them in the German school would allow them to adjust more easily to their new life. As for English, they would get enough exposure in their everyday life.

They found a suitable flat in an apartment complex, about ten minutes away by car from the school. They looked into leasing options for a family car, with the help of the relocation agent. The agent would also take care of the paperwork, so that all they'd have to do was register with the local authorities as soon as they arrived.

The company put them in touch with another colleague from Germany who had moved to Singapore two years earlier with his family, and they exchanged emails asking for information on the healthcare system, getting recommendations for a paediatrician and even a child psychologist. One of their sons was very introverted and they worried about him having trouble adjusting to a completely new culture and language.

They moved in early July. The boys were excited to be going on such a long trip and being allowed to watch as many movies as they wanted on the plane. During packing, their parents allowed them to pick their favourite books and toys and pack their own boxes. They also gave them each a small backpack, in which they put their favourite stuffed animals and objects that they would take with them on the plane.

Sabine and Alex did all the right things. They identified key issues, discussed the move in-depth, created a plan, involved the children, visited the country beforehand and engaged help. Even with all of their preparation, however, they still missed some key points.

## COMMON MISTAKES

Few expats do as good a job planning and preparing as Sabine and Alex. Many make common mistakes, resulting in moves that are unnecessarily difficult and disruptive:

1. **Not identifying key focus areas upfront.** Too often, assignees and their families don't spend enough time doing

an inventory of the full set of implications – key choices and focus areas – of relocation. As a result, they are not able to prioritize their efforts and so don't get off to a good start. Others prioritize dealing with the basics of accommodation, finances or other practical aspects, and neglect to factor in the family's wellbeing. Sabine and Alex were systematic in tackling key practical concerns before the move, but dropped the ball on understanding the rhythms of life in Singapore and building up their social network in advance. This left them feeling isolated during their first few weeks in Singapore: the boys did not start school until mid-August, and most other expat families were gone for the summer vacation.

2. **Underestimating the challenges.** Even seasoned expats can underestimate a move, often because they overestimate their ability to adjust. Jan, a Dutch diplomat, had lived in many different places, including India and the Middle East, but had the hardest time adjusting to the United States. Having travelled to the US and being fluent in English, he made the mistake of assuming he knew American culture. Once there, however, he found everyday life confusing. He struggled to understand cultural nuances, and that undermined his ability to function effectively at work.

3. **Not giving enough consideration to concepts of home.** Feeling adjusted after an international move essentially means feeling at home. Not considering what each person who moves needs to feel at home provides no real foundation for planning. Canadian expat Alison struggled in the spacious new apartment her husband had found for them prior to her arrival in Bratislava. To Alison, it felt old and dark, and was almost impossible to make 'homey' because it was already furnished. She regretted not having discussed expectations and priorities with her husband when they were preparing for the move.

Beyond helping you avoid common mistakes, this chapter will show you how to establish a solid planning foundation by focusing on the right areas and identifying the resources you need to make a great move.

## HOW TO PLAN AND PREPARE FOR A MOVE

If you have the opportunity to use the services of a relocation specialist or other assistance provided by your employer (for example, cross-cultural training), take advantage of it. Even with specialized assistance, though, you will still need to manage and undertake a lot of planning and preparation yourself. From the detailed task list presented below, select the areas most relevant to your particular circumstances and needs. These are not necessarily meant to be taken in sequence, though it is important to start with the first one.

### Identify the Most Important Choices You Need to Make

Start by identifying the key focus areas and choices that you (and your family, if applicable) will need to make, depending on your particular circumstances and needs. The most common areas are:

- Timing
- Housing
- Schooling
- Support network

Identify the key focus areas, then prioritize them. Break up broad priorities into smaller tasks, then build a checklist of what needs to be done by whom and when, depending on the timing of your move.

As you go through the choices, identify essential resources – what you need, what you have and what you need to get –

for each phase of the move. It's important to be proactive: pay attention early to what kind of support your employer is providing or could potentially provide. Many employers are open to negotiating reasonable needs and concerns.

## Assess the Trade-offs and Challenges

Be prepared to make tough trade-offs. For example, putting kids in local schools may benefit their language skills, but could make their initial adjustment tougher. Likewise, if you decide to socialize only with other expats, you will most likely benefit from immediate support from people who know exactly what you are going through, but may not take advantage of fully immersing yourself in the culture of your new home. Be aware of and acknowledge the trade-offs each key choice involves.

As you do this, take care to anticipate the challenges of transition, practical and emotional, for each family member. This will help you think about how to support them – and yourself – in coping with these challenges. As discussed in Chapter 2, some adjustment challenges will be linked to aspects of personality and experience. It is important to acknowledge them so that you can help yourself and your family develop coping mechanisms.

Be realistic about the amount of time you will need to take care of move logistics and to settle into your new home. Again, if you are moving with a partner, anticipate and be clear about your availability during the transition and the contributions you will be able make. If work will consume you for your first few months in a new role, then everyone needs to understand and plan for that. Make sure your partner has support to compensate for your absence, for example, by flying over a parent or relative to help out during the initial period of settling in.

Last, think carefully about what you (and each of your loved ones) need to create a real sense of home in the new location.

## Think About Timing

One key trade-off concerns timing. Do you all move together at the same time – and when? Or should the assignee move first, while the family follows later – and when? Do you have a choice? There are pros and cons associated with every approach.

Moving without the family allows the assignee to focus on getting up to speed in their new position during the first few months. "It's easier to invest the time and focus on your new job if you don't have someone waiting for you at home," said Norbert, a German expat who moved to Warsaw ahead of his wife and daughter. When they finally arrived, six months later, he was able to help them get settled, since he was already settled at work. At the same time, having the assignee move first can be a lonely experience, leave the partner struggling to cope as a single parent and the children missing their mother or father for a certain period of time. Having your partner and family with you when you move provides you with a built-in support system, both practical and emotional. You have someone to share the logistics of moving, but also to share your excitement and frustrations as you go through the normal adjustment cycle. And you also have the foundation of your social life right there, and don't have to feel isolated and lonely, especially in the first few months.

## Prepare the Paperwork

As soon as possible, you should make a list of all your administrative requirements. If you are working with a relocation specialist, be clear about the kinds of services that are included in your package. Most relocation service providers should help you figure out the following. If not, you will need to figure them out on your own as soon as possible.

1. **Residence and work permits.** Start early on these. What documents do you need to register with the authorities of the new place? If you are moving with your spouse/family,

what are the requirements for them? Are there restrictions for accompanying spouses as far as employment is concerned? If you have pets, have you checked quarantine and other requirements for them in the new location?

2.  **Financial and tax matters.** Be sure you understand the financial implications of your move. Clarify your tax status in the new location, particularly if you have ties, such as property or income, from another location. Seek the advice of a professional (a financial adviser or tax accountant familiar with international tax and legal frameworks) early on in the planning process.

3.  **Cost-of-living assessment.** It's easy to underestimate the cost of living in the new country.[1] Be sure to have a big enough 'cushion' in your budget to provide for potential cost-of-living increases after the move, as well as for potential exchange-rate fluctuations. Take care to factor in the impact of obligations or income that comes in a different currency than that of your new location (e.g., having to repay a loan in a different currency than that of your salary). Remember you are not a tourist anymore, so don't spend like you are on vacation.

4.  **Medical matters.** Does your current health insurance cover you in the new location and, if so, what specifically does it cover? Do you need to secure a new insurance policy locally – public, private, both? If you have dependants, what coverage do they need in the new location? Do you have copies of your medical records to take with you? Are there any medical requirements/vaccinations that you need to take care of before you move? Is there medication that you take regularly and of which you need to ensure adequate supply in the new location?

5.  **Other types of insurance.** Car, home, accident and other types of insurance are also important. As you wind down your insurance policies in the country you are leaving, set them up immediately in the new one.

6. **Banking and other financial matters.** If it is possible before the actual move, set up a bank account at your destination to take care of local and recurring expenses (rent, utilities).

Make copies of all the important documents – passports, visas, proofs of citizenship, birth/marriage/divorce/other certificates, driver's licenses, insurance and social security cards, employment records, income tax returns, medical records, school records, will(s) and powers of attorney – and keep them in a safe place, shielded from the chaos of the move. You may even want to consider scanning the documents and saving them in an app or the hard drive of your computer.

## Visit, If You Can

A 'look-see' visit helps you get a sense of what life will be like in your new location, gives your expectations a reality check, and allows you to fine-tune your planning. Do your homework before you go. Set aside at least two, but ideally four, days. If there is jet lag involved, you might want to give yourself an additional day or two. To prepare for the visit you should:

1. Have a detailed agenda and itinerary. Structuring your days will help you make the most of your time. Decide on the places you need to visit (schools, potential homes, government agencies) and make appointments. Some of those appointments may need to be made well in advance, so start early.
2. Figure out locations (work, potential schools and homes) and distances. It is essential to take this into consideration both for setting up and scheduling your short visit, and in making final decisions about where you will live. Budget enough time for each appointment, taking into account distances and transportation options.

3. Be prepared to focus on the right things, such as:
   a. Prospective homes and their proximity to work and/ or schools.
   b. Prospective schools.
   c. The infrastructure around prospective homes: food stores, shops, banks, restaurants, hospitals (and distances), pharmacies, sports and other facilities (public transport, railways and/or airport).
   d. The public transportation system. 'Test drive' it if you have the time. You will get a better feel for distances and how long you need to get places.
   e. The character of neighbourhoods and their friendliness to expats.

As you think things through, imagine yourself living there and anticipate what your needs will be. Do your background research before you go. Government, travel and expat sites, blogs and forums offer a lot of useful information. If you have any contacts in the new location, get in touch and ask for advice. It helps to know in advance, for example, what the requirements are for renting a property in the new location (paperwork, deposits).

## Find a Home

Start by expanding and then narrowing your options: House or apartment? Rent or buy? How big? City or country? Close to schools? Close to work? If you are moving with a family, try to get everyone on the same page with respect to at least the key criteria, then start looking from afar.

Think through what compromises you are prepared to make. If you or your spouse are city people, but your kids want a home with a garden, you may have to settle for moving to a suburb. If you are working with a relocation or real estate agent, be as precise as possible about your needs as a family and how you imagine your new home. Sometimes standards and tastes differ by culture. For example, an apartment that is considered spacious enough for a family in Manhattan, where living spaces tend to be smaller on average, is very different than the equivalent in Barcelona.

Sometimes it is hard to make the right call if you have not visited the place to which you are moving. If you can, visit and look at homes. Get a feel for different neighbourhoods and which ones feel most like home. Think of your lifestyle and try to imagine what it will be like living there. If you are an avid runner, is there a park nearby where you can go for your daily jog?

When Jennifer, an American diplomatic spouse, moved to Vienna with her family, they decided to take an apartment in the suburbs, following a recommendation by their embassy, because it was close to her husband's work. Later, she regretted that decision. "I felt very isolated. We should have lobbied the embassy so that we could have lived closer to the city centre, but at the time we did not know we would want that or that it was an option."

What if you can't visit? There's still a lot you can do. There are many more possibilities for searching from a distance than there were even five years ago. Use map applications to look at different areas and neighbourhoods. Talk to people online who live or have lived there to get a sense of what your daily life will be like and get other information.

In order to make your new place into a home, it is important to maintain continuity and a sense of comfort through familiar elements, such as furniture and other possessions. Ascertain the extent to which the company will pay for you to move your personal goods. Do you have a fixed allowance for moving and have to choose what comes with you? Or do you pay for your own move? In any case, what elements are important for you to take with you in your new home? Plan for that, whether it's your furniture, your family pictures, pieces of art or other. Continuity is particularly important when moving with children. For example, it helps to engage your children in planning what to have in their personal space so that they feel at home.

## Start Building Your Support Network

According to a survey of 500 expats worldwide by global healthcare company AXA PPP International, 40% of respondents considered being away from their support network as one of the most difficult aspects of transition to life abroad.[2] Lack of good support can lead to increased stress and feelings of isolation, among others. Therefore, it pays to be proactive and begin to build your new support system before you go. This is crucial if only one of you will be the one doing the bulk of the work setting up your family's support structures.

Start by identifying your sources of support. This includes institutions (childcare, healthcare), routines (schedules, activities), and people (friends, colleagues, other expats, caregivers, teachers, doctors, other service providers). Identify the type of support each can offer you.

People are your most valuable resource. Start with friends or acquaintances who live in the new locations – especially other expats, who have faced similar challenges – or reach out to expat forums and organizations. Ask your employer's human resources department to connect you with colleagues who have previously moved to your destination or are still there.

Beyond that, identify potential communities where you (and your partner and/or children) would naturally feel connected and supported. If you have a favourite sport or hobby, look for clubs or associations that you could join. If you want to be near other expats or other like-minded people, find out where those communities are located – both physically and online. If you have a relocation agent, ask for their help in identifying those communities.

Healthcare is also key. You want to understand whether the new location could exacerbate existing health challenges.

Figure out what you need to access healthcare and ideally have a list of key doctors who speak your native language or at least a language in which you are conversant, maybe even have some appointments set up before you move. You never know what may come up and how fast you may need support. Moves are usually stressful and can affect your health.

The high air pollution levels in Beijing, combined with the stress of her move there from Argentina, exacerbated Maria's allergies dramatically. She had not had the chance to find a primary care physician before she moved, so she ended up having to go to the emergency room at the local hospital just to be able to have a doctor see her.

If you have children, especially if you plan on working right away in your new location, researching childcare options, and having some lined up before you move is crucial to avoiding unnecessary stress and struggle during the moving and settling phase.

## Anticipate Additional Support Needs

What would you need beyond the basics? When Patricia moved to Brazil for her husband's job, having heard that car-jacking was not uncommon and concerned about the safety of her children being driven to the international school, she requested (and got from their employer) an armoured car with bulletproof windows.

Take advantage of the resources provided by your employer, but also be proactive about obtaining additional resources. Does your employer provide expenses or an allowance that you can allocate according to your needs (e.g., career coaching for your partner)? Here are examples of additional support that you may need to arrange for.

### Language training

Among the many expats I interviewed, one of the top regrets was not learning the local language early enough. Even if you will not need the local language at the office, it is still valuable to learn it. If you don't understand the language, you will miss the cultural nuances that are expressed through it, which are important when you do business in a different culture. If you are the accompanying spouse, language lessons could vastly simplify your daily life and provide a much-needed source of regular social connection at a time when you may feel isolated. The faster you become comfortable in the language of your new home, the sooner you will be able to function, understand the culture and become integrated.

Find out if your organization offers language training. Start at least six months before you move (even if your work will be in another language). If your partner or family are moving with you, they should start too.

## Cross-cultural training

Similar to language competence, cultural competence can have a big impact on how well you function in your new environment, increasing your confidence and reducing stress levels. Cross-cultural training familiarizes you with culture shock and the stages of adaptation, and helps you build the necessary skills to deal with cultural differences. It often includes practical information about the daily life and culture of the new place, knowledge that can reduce the stress of fig-uring out how things work the hard way. It also may give you insight into how business gets done at your destination (val-uable even if you are moving within an organization or speak the local language), which will help you be more effective at work. While cross-cultural training will not solve all your problems, or guarantee a smooth adjustment, it will most likely make adjustment less stressful than it otherwise would be. Cross-cultural training is particularly important when the new culture is very different from your home culture.

Many employers now offer some form of cultural aware-ness training as part of relocation support, often extending that to spouses and children. Ideally, the whole family should benefit from such training. A follow-up, post-arrival training also is extremely helpful, as it allows you to ask the questions that inevitably come up as you are settling in. Ask for such support even if you are familiar with the culture and language of your destination. Only Sofia's Austrian husband was offered cross-cultural training when they moved to Argentina. His employer assumed that she didn't need it since she was Spanish and spoke the language. Once there, however, Sofia felt out of place and struggled to adjust.

**Psychological support for you and your family**
Your family may benefit from emotional support with the process of transition, such as counselling from a qualified professional who speaks your language. As discussed, people handle transitions in different ways. You may feel isolated and lonely. Your spouse may have just had a baby and be struggling with post-partum depression around the time that culture shock hits. Your teenage son may have trouble integrating into his new high school. It is important to have resources in case such support is needed before, during and especially after you've made the move.

**Ongoing relocation support**
Consider asking your employer for ongoing relocation support, at least for the first year of your move. This is especially valuable if you are the accompanying partner and have to manage setting up your daily life and support network, while dealing with the language barrier, local bureaucracy and culture shock.

Asking for and getting all this extra support can have a powerful impact on how your move goes. Providing the expat partner and children with the support they need will not only help them make a smoother transition, but it will also allow the assignee to focus more on settling into their new position at work.

## Prioritize Your Relationship

It is crucial to support each other through the planning phase. Discuss and agree on the detailed plan for the move. Make sure that you are both involved in all decisions related to the move, such as the details of relocation policies and benefits, immigration and work permit details. Often information is communicated to the working expatriate and not to their partner, who may, in fact, be the one handling the logistics of the move.

An international move inevitably puts stress on relationships, so be prepared. A strong bond is a solid source of emotional support throughout this challenging process. Empathy, openness and communication can go a long way towards making the move go smoother. Make time for each other. Check in regularly and be open with each other about your feelings during this transition – both positive and negative. Acknowledge and show appreciation. Address unresolved relationship issues *before* you move.

## Support the Children

Involve your children in planning, to the extent possible given their ages. Discuss options with them, listen to their opinions and arguments, and give them real choices. Keep them in the loop, but don't overwhelm them with information, especially if they are too young to process it. Involving your children will make them feel useful and taken seriously. Even more important, it will give them a sense of control over their lives in a process that was not their decision. Finally, it will get them more interested and invested in the idea of the move, which in turn will help them adjust more easily.

Here are some areas where your children could get involved:

1. If possible, ask for their input on the timing of the move.
2. Assign them specific tasks. The internet can be a handy

research tool. When we were planning our move to Zurich, our ten-year-old son was responsible for figuring out distances and connections between potential neighbourhoods and schools using the local transport network.

3. Involve them in evaluating schools, but clarify with them in advance whether they get to make the final choice. If you cannot take them with you to visit schools, go on the school websites or look at their promotional material together.

4. Involve them in the choice of neighbourhood and housing, to the extent possible.

5. Have them pack their own boxes, depending on their age. Create a box with favourite objects for each child, a sort of 'comfort box' to be unpacked first.

6. Ask them what they want their rooms to look like, so that they have a sense of control and something to look forward to.

7. Have them research and pick after-school activities. Clarify what is non-negotiable (for us, it was Greek and music lessons).

8. Talk with your children about what their new life will be like. Go into detail. Look at pictures together or look up information online. Find out what inspires or excites them and could help with adjustment. Sabine and Alex promised their sons that they would be able to continue playing football, their favourite sport, in Singapore.

Last, but not least, throughout the planning phase (but also through all the other phases) keep open the lines of communication. Allow your children to express their full range of feelings about the move. Are they worried about making new friends, leaving behind their loved ones, managing in a new language, going to a new school? Discuss and acknowledge these as real concerns. Reassure them that you will support them.

## A Word on School Choice

When choosing a school, consider the set of criteria: local, international, bilingual, national (in your native language)? Would your child benefit from a smaller, more intimate setting or is a bigger school more fitting to their personality? What can you afford? Should the school be close to your home or are you also willing to consider options farther away? Does it make sense to find the school first and then the home or the other way around? If you have teenagers, it may make sense to also think about higher education options down the road.

If you visit prospective schools, is it possible to bring the children with you? Talk to parents whose children go to the school you are considering. Most schools are happy to provide contacts, and parents usually are eager to help newcomers. Knowing some families at your children's future school before you move will help with their social integration once you're there (for starters, you will have people to set up play dates).

When choosing the type of school, factor in the fit with your child's personality. Also, consider what makes sense given your long-term time horizon. If your assignment only lasts two years, you may not want to put your child in a local school and have them go through the process of learning a new language – or you may decide that it would be their one chance to be fully immersed in the local culture. It is important to think about what comes next and what kind of school will maintain continuity for your child. If your child has a learning difficulty or disability, consider choosing one system that you will be able to maintain in future moves. If that is not possible locally, and depending on your child's age, boarding school may be an alternative for maintaining continuity.

Especially if the new school system will be different than the one they are used to, you need to prepare your children by explaining the differences, whether in terms of language, curriculum, academic level, testing, grading or the cultural (or religious) values transmitted. Reassure them that you will support them in every way you can, including getting them counselling or tutoring and being in direct contact with their new school and teachers to make this transition as smooth as possible for them. Don't forget that if your children will be taught in a language that you don't speak, you will not be able to help them with their schoolwork.

## Build the Foundations of Home

Throughout the book, I have emphasized the importance of creating home, in its various forms, at your new location. To accelerate this process, research your destination. Learn as much as you can about the landscape, climate, history, politics, people, social norms and values. Listen to the music. Taste the food. Explore the art. Try to experience the depth of the culture while still at home. Get a sense of what your daily life will be like. Building this familiarity will help you create a sense of home much faster.

Emma, an American living in Vienna, wished she had not waited so long to learn about Austrian history. "I wish I had done it earlier, because it helped me understand better the mentality of the people, the customs, the way the society is set up – and ultimately to feel more comfortable living there." Leo Tolstoy said that "Understanding everything is forgiving everything."

You gain a lot by doing traditional research (books, newspaper or magazine articles, expat blogs and websites, news, radio, TV, podcasts), but people often are your most valuable resource. Talk to those who live or have lived there – future colleagues, friends of friends, other expats. Tell everyone where you're going; they may well know someone there. Reach out to expat organizations and forums for referrals and advice on dealing with practical needs, such as understanding recycling rules or how to register your child at the local school.

As you do your research, think of the elements of your current life that you would like to include into your new life. What will you miss the most? Is it your house, your rituals, the food, the music? Research will help you identify the best ways to maintain a connection to the elements of home that mean most to you – a cultural centre, a shop selling products from your home country, a language course for your children or an expatriate community that you can join.

If rituals and routines are an important part of home, think about how to maintain continuity in the new location. Laying the groundwork before you move will be helpful when you are settling in and overwhelmed with the adjustment process. Maybe it's important to find the closest gym, a place where you can practice your favourite hobby, or a nice café where you can read the Sunday paper. In particular, family rituals help you stay connected, especially through the transition, and feel at home faster.

However much research you do, though, be sure to keep an open mind. It's great to have an idea what to expect, but your perceptions may change when you experience the new culture up close. Be prepared for that.

Finally, organize something to look forward to for you and your family. Identify a few activities or places to visit soon after you arrive at your destination. This will help you get to know your new home, but also start the new adventure on a positive note and get everyone excited about the impending move.

## Anticipate the Career Impact

Going back to Sabine and Alex from the beginning of this chapter, Alex knew that, in order to be able to get back to work in Singapore, he would need a resume and interview training specific to the local culture. He also would need to work with an executive coach familiar with the Singaporean job market for at least a few months before starting to look for a job. Sabine negotiated this into her contract.

Whether your partner plans to be professionally active in the new location, take a career break, stay at home, engage in volunteer or charity work or make other choices, actively help them get the support they need. This is especially important if they are giving up a job or even a career they love to follow you. Helping your partner manage their professional transition not only enhances the odds of success of your relocation, it also benefits your relationship. Making this move for the benefit of your career is a joint project, so invest in making sure that your partner finds fulfilment, professionally or otherwise.

If your partner aspires to find work in the new location, you should:

1. Clarify the legal framework and documentation necessary for doing so (visa, work permit, legal framework for setting up a business, if relevant). Identify potential barriers and address them early on.
2. Ascertain whether your employer provides career development assistance to expat partners (increasingly they do). If so, get information on the types of support available and actively help your partner get it. This could be an education allowance, support with their job search, training for resume preparation and/or interviewing and other kinds of assistance.
3. If your partner cannot continue their career, does not have a specific idea what they want to do or is in the process of reinventing him- or herself, career counselling or coaching, specialized training or other resources may be useful.

Regardless, take the time to discuss how their career can benefit from this move, not just yours. Be proactive about helping them secure that support. Be interested and involved in the process.

If your partner is planning to stay at home, help them get connected socially so they don't feel isolated. Explore the expat or school community.

For partners who seek to be professionally active, help them to focus on identifying the options they want to pursue.

Wendy, an Australian advertising executive who quit her job to follow her husband to the Philippines, thought she would find another job in no time. A first-time expat, she arrived in Manila without having done any background research and found that not to be the case. First, it was not as easy to get a work permit as she had expected. Second, she could hardly find anything suitable in her field. And third, even the very few positions she could apply for paid extremely low salaries compared to what she earned previously. She was extremely frustrated and resented not being able to work.

It's much harder to adjust if you don't think things through. However, even if you are aware that there will be consequences, be prepared for a larger-than-expected impact on your wellbeing and sense of identity. Ask for support, if needed.

If you're the one accompanying your partner, and you plan to look for a job in your new location, do the following before you move:

1. **Research the job market at your destination**
   - Get a good understanding of the local recruitment processes and practices.
   - Find out whether your qualifications are transferable in the new location and if not, or if they are only partly transferable, understand what steps you need to take to remedy that.
   - Check whether you need to get your credentials approved or need additional qualifications.
2. **Make yourself more marketable**
   - Get your paperwork in order, according to your findings in 1.

- Get career support either before or after the move. For example, get assistance with your CV/resume, interviewing, networking and presentation techniques. If possible, get support in defining and honing your marketable skills for the specific market. This kind of support should also offer insight into the cultural specifics of the recruitment process in the local job market. For instance, it should allow you to update and adapt your CV to meet local requirements.

3. **Jumpstart building your network**
   - Reach out or ask to be introduced to professional networks in your field.
   - If you plan on returning home and continuing your career there, maintain your network, stay knowledgeable about your field and keep your skills up to date.

As you evaluate your options, keep the time frame in mind. Depending on how long the assignment will be, and/or whether there are follow-up assignments on the horizon, what do you expect the impact to be on your professional identity and options? How will the assignment affect your career prospects, long-term earnings potential, financial independence and pension contributions? Armed with insight into your goals, identify the resources that you have and those that you will need to build up or seek. Be explicit. Many of those resources can be, and ideally are, negotiated into the acceptance of the assignment.

## Lay the Foundations for Finding Your Tribe

Start building your social network before you move. Making friends is among the top concerns of people who relocate, particularly single movers. If you wait until you are at your destination and overwhelmed with the process of adjustment, you will not have the time or energy to give your social life the focus and attention it deserves. Making some connections before you arrive, even having a few meetings scheduled, will help you avoid becoming isolated during that crucial initial time.

What can you do for your social network in advance of the move? Look for supportive, like-minded communities. Research – even join – clubs or groups, such as professional associations, organizations with an expat focus or clubs organized around an activity or interest, hobby, or sport that you like. Most countries or cities have at least one expat organization, and there are also global ones that are active in various countries around the world, such as Internations.[3] Meetup[4] groups are also a big resource, based in multiple geographical locations and built around particular interests of their members. There are also many online forums. Look for activities that you are already pursuing or pick something that you have always wanted to do.

People are your most valuable resource and having the foundations of a network will help you (and your family) tremendously with adjustment. Unfortunately, Sabine and Alex did not think about seeking out connections ahead of their move, with the result that, once Sabine was at work and especially later, when the boys started school, Alex found himself isolated. In his case, as a male expat partner, he had a hard time finding a community of other expats. Most of the networks and events in the expat community were targeted to women (the majority of expat partners). Alex felt excluded and that made his adjustment much more challenging.

After three years in Singapore, Sabine was offered another expat assignment, this time in New York. It was a promotion and too good to pass up, so they decided to go for it. However, what started as a one-off 'Asian adventure' turned into an expat-track career neither of them had expected or planned for. Sabine had not really discussed her long-term career plan with her manager when she was offered the initial move to Singapore. Alex had not thought about the career implications for him of such a lifestyle either, and the two of them had not discussed the implications for their family. For instance, they might have made different schooling choices to maintain continuity by sending the boys to an international school in Singapore. The German school in their new posting was far from Manhattan where Sabine's work was, so they had to send them to an American school. Adjusting to a new culture and school in a language in which they were not fluent resulted in the boys struggling for a while, just as they were at the doorstep of puberty.

In the **Appendix**, I provide an example of how to organize and manage your list of decisions and tasks (what – who – by when) when preparing and executing your move. I hope it inspires you to make your own list, tailored to your unique circumstances and needs. There is only so much you can anticipate when you prepare for a move, which, by definition, is filled with uncertainty. However, if you follow the systematic approach I describe in this chapter, you can maximize your odds of success. As Benjamin Franklin said, "Failing to plan is planning to fail."

# CHECKLIST

- What are the most important choices you need to make to prepare for your move? What are the biggest trade-offs associated with those choices?

- What is the right timing for the move and what are the implications for every member of the family?

- Have you identified all the paperwork and other legal and regulatory requirements for making the move? Do you have a plan for completing them?

- Have you established priorities for rebuilding your support network at the new location? Are there additional sources of support you will need and, if so, how will you secure them?

- What will you do to be sure you preserve your relationship, support the children, and rebuild home during this challenging time?

- Have you thought through the implications of the move for both partners' careers and identified options and strategies for the accompanying partner to thrive in the new location?

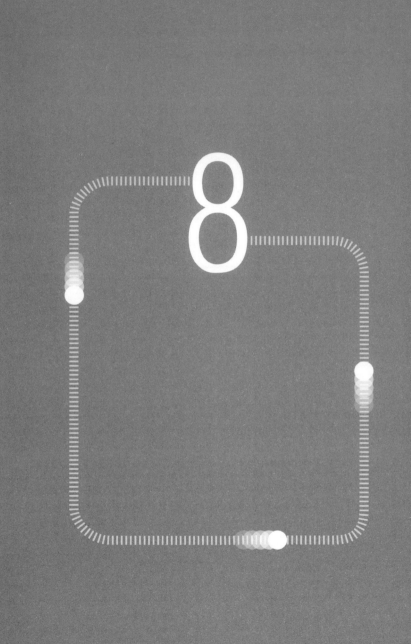

8

MOVING

*"How lucky I am to have something that makes saying goodbye so hard."*

**Winnie the Pooh**

Regardless of how much preparation you do, moving to a new country can feel overwhelming and unexpected events may still come your way. It's easy to think that making the move is just about the logistics of getting your stuff to the new location. However, there are also many crucial emotional aspects of leaving one life and transitioning to another that you need to take into account.

Karin met John in Munich when she was working there as an au pair. She's Austrian, from Vienna, and he's American, from Seattle. He'd been transferred to Germany by the online retailer for whom he worked. They dated, got married and had two daughters. Karin decided to stay home to raise them. When their daughters were two and four years old, John received an offer to transfer back to headquarters in the US. Karin had visited the US before as a tourist, and was excited at the idea of living in Seattle. They were in their late 20s at the time, and for Karin it was her first international move. They did not give it much thought or planning, except for organizing the packing process.

John got the offer in late fall and they decided to move together in the new year. Karin felt that it was best not to tell their girls too early about the impending move. It would shield them from the stress of moving, she thought, and she was unsure about how to explain the move to them at such a young age. John agreed and they decided to tell the girls four days before the movers were due to show up.

They decided to take their daughters to the US once before the move, reasoning that it would help them get used to the new location, so during the Christmas vacation, they flew to Seattle. They spent three weeks there with John's family and visited the apartment they had rented. Karin remembers, "We thought that would help them feel comfortable once we moved. Now they knew the apartment, what more would they need? They were only two and four, after all."

Back in Munich, the movers came and packed everything. Karin and the girls stayed a few nights with friends, while John flew to Seattle to start his new position. The plan was to follow him a week later. A few days before their flight to the US, Karin realized she had misplaced her and the girls' passports. They had to delay their departure by ten days to have time to apply for new emergency travel documents.

Karin had decided that the three of them needed a break from all the stress of the move and had planned a stopover in Boston to visit her sister who was studying there. That way, she thought, the girls would get used to the new time zone gradually, and the three of them could recharge their batteries before they had to start unpacking in Seattle. However, soon after they arrived at their new home, the girls started showing signs of distress.

## COMMON MISTAKES

The experience of Karin and John isn't an unusual one. Even well-intentioned parents may not recognize the vast difference between moving alone versus moving with a family, and so set themselves up for failure. Compared to other phases, such as deciding whether to move or preparing to go, the actual physical act of moving seems deceptively straightforward. It's easy to think that it's just about organizing and transporting your belongings from point A to point B. Common mistakes include:

1. **Not saying proper goodbyes.** Many expats become too focused on logistics and neglect the emotional aspects of moving. Karin and John did not give their daughters the time to say goodbye to their old life. While they thought they were protecting them by not sharing the news until the last minute, in reality they did not allow the girls time to get used to the idea or to take leave from favourite people and places. As a result, their daughters went through a period of intense sadness after moving, which lasted several months. Especially their eldest felt homesick and missed her friends from kindergarten in Munich. Convincing her to go to her new kindergarten in Seattle was a daily struggle.

2. **Not thinking ahead when packing.** Due to either lack of time or other priorities (such as managing the administrative details of arriving in the new country), many expats don't take enough time to sort through their belongings thoughtfully before moving them, and instead rely on the moving company to do all the work. Karin and John did no preparation before the movers showed up. Had they taken some time to go through their belongings and decide what stayed with them and what went in the container, they would not have realized, long after the fact, that the movers had packed a folder with important documents – including the passports for Karin and their daughters.

3. **Not pacing yourself.** A move is a marathon, but too many treat it like a sprint. You go through a very intense period making the decision, and then preparing and planning your move. By the time you are done packing, stress levels are likely to be high and energy levels low. But you still need strength for the equally demanding phase of making the move and getting unpacked. Mary Ann worked really

hard before her move from New Jersey to London and did a good job setting everything up. She thought the movers would pack on one end and unpack on the other, and her work would be done. She did not expect that, even with the movers' help, the whole process would take so much time and energy. By the time she found herself amidst her unpacked boxes in her new home, she was exhausted and dreaded starting her new job the next day.

## LEAVE WELL SO YOU CAN ARRIVE WELL

A rocky departure sets the stage for unnecessary confusion and stress. Sometimes the decision to move or the announcement of an impending move happens on such short notice that you do not have enough time to internalize what it means for you or to achieve sufficient closure. Whether you have to move quickly or have plenty of time, however, strive to focus on these critical elements:

### Give Notice and Resolve Outstanding Issues

Give timely notices, where necessary, in advance of your move. Notify your landlord, if you are renting, as well as utility and telephone companies, and the children's schools. Cancel any non-transferrable contracts (for instance, mobile phones), health insurance, gym and other memberships and subscriptions. Think about who needs to know your new address. Arrange for your mail to be forwarded as soon as you have a forwarding address.

As soon as possible, you also should sort out any outstanding business, obligations or commitments – such as work projects, non-transferrable financial obligations, outstanding bills that still need to be paid from the new location or other commitments. Check requirements for ensuring the validity of your driver's license in the new location. Most countries allow you a grace period for abiding by those requirements.

Finally, arrange for temporary accommodation at your new location, such as hotel reservations or short-term residence arrangements, until your house or apartment is available and/or your stuff arrives.

## Plan Your Goodbyes

As you prepare for your move, try to budget enough time in the departure phase to bid your farewells. Create a list of people, places and activities that are important to you and think about how you will say goodbye. Throw a goodbye party, if you can. Make it memorable.

If you are moving with children, give them the chance to say goodbye to important people and places in their lives. Arrange for them to see their close friends, having as many play dates and sleepovers as possible. Organize a farewell party, and allow your children to choose where they want it to be, and who should be there. Take them to their favourite spots – parks, restaurants, the ice cream parlour – and engage in favourite activities with them for the last time.

In our last few weeks in Vienna before we moved to Zurich, we went to the children's favourite Austrian restaurant for one last Wiener Schnitzel and to the famous *Prater* amusement park for a ride on the giant Ferris wheel. The week before we packed up, our children had a joint farewell party where they invited all their friends. Everyone had fun, even though the atmosphere was also a little melancholic. Our kids were thrilled to have all their favourite people there. We took lots of pictures.

## Collect or Create Keepsakes

Giving yourself and your children something to hold on to helps with homesickness and the sense of loss you will experience during transition. Having sacred objects with you at the right moments can be comforting and reassuring: a favourite picture, a teddy bear, a much-loved sweater, a faded blanket.

They are part of your history; a reminder, as well as a link with your previous lives that you can bring to your new life.

Pictures, albums or scrapbooks are also invaluable for keeping memories alive, especially for younger children who may have a hard time remembering their 'old' life after a while. Our move to Zurich was our first move with the children. Before we left Vienna, I took pictures of our family, our neighbourhood, our friends and our children's friends, and used them to create a 'Vienna Album' for each of our children, with photos from their life there. To this day, they love going back and browsing through those albums, which are important reminders of their life stories.

If the stress of the move does not allow you to create something like that, friends may be more than happy to do it for you. Our daughter's school friends made her a friendship book, in which they all wrote. Scrapbooks and albums are great for preserving memories, but you can also be creative with other kinds of objects. We had our son's friends write dedications on a map of Vienna and asked our daughter's friends to sign her Taekwondo belt, both of which they could hang up in their respective new rooms.

## Plan How You Will Stay in Touch

Agree how you will stay in contact with family and friends that you are leaving behind. Knowing by what means and how often you will be able to keep in touch can make the transition a little smoother for you, for those you're saying goodbye to and especially for your children. Having your loved ones' support will help your children with the adjustment. It will also provide your friends and family with some comfort that you will not suddenly disappear from their lives. Here are some ways you can plan for that:

1. Make sure you have defined channels for staying connected. Send out your new contact details and update

everyone's contacts. Connect on social media and set up social media groups. Start a family blog to keep your friends and family updated.

2. Proactively plan to set up the technology infrastructure that your family and friends will use to keep in touch. Many expats equip their parents or other relatives with tablets and laptops. They set up email, social media and video communication accounts for them and teach them how to use them.

3. Help your children, especially the young ones, stay in touch with their friends. Coordinate with the other parents and encourage them to also support that communication. Model the importance of nurturing friendships by making an effort to stay connected with your own friends.

4. Plan for people to come visit you and/or organize your first trip back. Many expats find that it helps to plan that first trip before they even move, because it gives everyone something to look forward to. However, be thoughtful about the timing of the return visit, especially if you have children. You need to balance your desire to comfort the pain of homesickness with the knowledge that, if they return to visit too soon after the move, it may cause them to regress just as they are starting to adjust to their new home.

## Pack Strategically

Now that we've covered the emotional packing process, let us tackle the practical side of getting the years of possessions strewn about your house sorted into boxes. Being systematic in your packing will save you a lot of time when you unpack. Here's how to do that.

### Clear out the clutter

Throw out, donate, sell. Every move is an opportunity to get rid of stuff you don't need, love or use regularly. Don't pay professionals to move junk from one place to another.

When Rosie moved from Toronto to Dubai for her new job, she had no time to plan the move. She hired her employer's preferred moving company and trusted that they would take care of all the packing. She arrived at her new home and started unpacking, only to find that the movers were so diligent in packing everything, that they also packed a garbage bag full of trash. Funny enough, Rosie's experience is one of the most common moving mishaps expats report.

### Anticipate what your new life will be like

Imagine being in your new home. Look around you and envision your possessions. Also, picture what your daily life will be like. With that vision, make a list of what you will need to take with you. What can't you live without? What's available in the new location and what will you need to import (The toaster? A cheese grater? Chocolate?). Will you be able to import household appliances? When we moved from the US back to Europe, because of the difference in voltage, we left behind all our lamps and other appliances.

Factor in the impact of changes in climate. Sabine and Alex, from the previous chapter, did not know how destructive Singapore's extremely humid atmosphere would be for their belongings. Barely a year into their assignment, their leather couch developed mould, as did their dining room table and chairs, framed paintings and family pictures. Even their computers and TV set were affected. They had to throw a lot away when it was time for their next move. If you are moving from Oslo to Bangkok, you may want to consider putting your ski gear and heavy winter coats in storage (don't do the same with the kids' snow suits, however; they will not fit them when you return, so it's better to sell or give those away). If the climate of your destination requires you to buy special clothing or equipment, research what you will need specifically, and look into buying things in advance and shipping them.

Your housing situation and your moving allowance (if relevant), will also influence what you take with you. Decide what is most important for you and your family to have with you in the new place. Make a list of what will come with you and what you will put in storage, sell or give away. For some it's books, for others kitchen- and dinnerware, family pictures or their children's art works. Put labels or sticky-notes on each piece of furniture that instruct the movers accordingly. If you are planning to buy furniture, make a list of what you will need, specifying dimensions and where it will go. The best way to go about that is to visit your new place and take measurements of all the rooms. Also, think about how your furniture will actually *enter* your flat or house. Is there a staircase or elevator and will all your furniture fit through those? Alternatively, ask the realtor or the owner for a plan of the place, and carefully think through and decide which piece of furniture fits where.

### If relevant, decide what will ship by what means

Depending on the destination and distance, you may have the option to send some belongings faster, by air, and others slower, by sea or land. Decide and make a list of what goes in each shipment. What will you need as soon as you get there? Put that in the suitcases that go with you. Other belongings that you will need as soon as possible (think of what would make your new living space immediately feel like home, such as pictures or other 'trademark' objects) should also be shipped by air. If you are moving during the winter season, for example, it makes sense to ship your winter clothes and gear by air, while your summer gear can arrive a little later, since you won't need it immediately. Karin and John did not take time to sort through their belongings. As a result, all their girls' belongings went into the 'slower' shipment, which took almost two months to get to Seattle. When the girls arrived in their new home, they had nothing to play with, no favourite toys or other objects to comfort them through the transition.

Take care not to inadvertently pack – or have the movers pack – critical documents, medications or other items that you should bring with you.

## Maintain Your Energy

Every phase of the move demands a lot of energy and attention. But it's hard to be focused and on the go the whole time. Learn to assess your energy levels, know what energizes you and recognize when you are heading for a low point. Think of yourself and your family members as having 'energy bank accounts'. Then be careful that you are not just making big withdrawals without commensurate deposits.

### Know when you need a break

Taking occasional breaks to renew your energy and recharge your batteries will help you stay fit and meet the demands of each phase. The greater the demands on you – for instance, if you are carrying most of the burden of the logistics of the move, or if you are having to both manage the move and perform at your new job – the more crucial it is to schedule some breaks to de-stress, unplug and relax. Set reminders on your phone, if you have to, and go for a walk, meet friends, get some exercise. Celebrate your accomplishments, however small. Maintain your sense of humour. Expect things to go wrong, to be different, ambiguous and uncertain.

If you can, take a break between the two sides of the move (or the packing and the unpacking) to recharge and do something good for yourself and your family. Visit family or friends, say your goodbyes, do something good for yourself.

### Practice self-care

It's easy to forget to stay connected to yourself and your loved ones when there is so much else going on that demands your attention. However, this is precisely the time you most need to do that, because self-awareness, self-care and connection with the people in your life are three keys to help you get through the challenging times and thrive through your transition.

Moving is stressful and so is adjusting to a new environment. That's why, at this time in your life, it is particularly important for you – and the whole family – to eat well, sleep enough and get sufficient exercise, so that you can stay healthy.

1. Regularly reminding yourself of the reasons you are making this move, especially at times when you feel overwhelmed, can be both soothing and energizing.
2. Be mindful of how your body reacts to stress. Headaches, irritability, insomnia, lethargy and other physical symptoms may be signs of distress or even depression. Take time regularly to pause and notice the signs of stress in your body, the way you breathe, which parts of you are tense and which are more relaxed.
3. Be attuned to your state of mind, your thoughts and emotions. You are likely to go through a roller-coaster of complex and often conflicting feelings. The more aware you are of those, the more grounded you will feel. Schedule regular time just for yourself, to do something that nourishes your spirit.
4. Have an outlet for stress, something to help you get rid of both physical and emotional tension. What works for you? Is it sports? Meditation? Going for a walk? Connecting with friends and family? Whatever it is, be proactive about scheduling it at regular intervals. For example, if yoga is your outlet for stress, establish a daily morning routine that includes it.
5. If things get rough, do not hesitate to ask for help from a qualified professional. Many expats are too overwhelmed by the process of the move to notice the symptoms of serious distress and wait too long to seek psychological support.

If you are moving with your family, be similarly mindful and alert to their needs and provide them with appropriate support.

## Don't Forget Your Relationships

If you are moving with your partner, make time for each other and stay connected. If one of you has to move earlier, it is even more important to nurture each other. It's easy for your relationship to take a back seat to everything else that's going on, especially if you are also physically distant. Keep communicating. As in every phase of the move, show empathy for each other's emotions and perspective, and be alert to each other's needs. Do not expect the other person to know what you are feeling. Check in regularly with each other on how you think the move is going. Ask for and offer support. Be a team. If you are the expatriate, budget enough time to go back and help your partner with the move. If they will be managing most of the logistics, acknowledge their contributions often and authentically. Don't be afraid to say when you're feeling unhappy, frustrated, overwhelmed or sad. Don't fall into the trap of expat guilt (the feeling that you are not allowed to be unhappy because you live a life of privilege).

Similar principles apply if you are moving with children. Check in with them regularly and stay attuned to their concerns. Observe their behaviour, be alert and watch for signs of distress. Your children inevitably will have mixed emotions about the move. They may also feel guilty about experiencing sadness, or reluctant to bother you when so much is going on. Encourage your children to express their emotions, acknowledge these without trying to 'fix' them. Let them know it's OK to be sad about leaving behind people, places and routines.

If feelings of loss and grief are left unexpressed, they are likely to resurface at a later point, most likely with higher intensity. It's important not to insulate them too much from hardship. On the contrary, coping with difficult emotions, with your support, will help them develop lifelong resilience.

It also helps if you are open and honest about your own feelings about the move, both the sadness of loss and the excitement of a new life. Nancy did that with her girls when they moved from Boston to Stockholm. "If they missed Boston, I said to them 'You know, I miss Boston sometimes too,' but then found something positive to say about Stockholm. Try to mean it, genuinely. Even on the days when you can't find a positive thing to say, you have to do it anyway."

Always keep in perspective what you have achieved already. It is probably much more than you think. And, again, hold on to your sense of humour. On challenging days, you are going to need it.

## CHECKLIST

- What do you need to do to make a good departure emotionally? What activities and people will help you (and your family, if applicable) say your goodbyes and make a graceful transition out of your old life?

- What sorts of objects, pictures and keepsakes will you use to remind yourself (especially your children) about the home you have left?

- Have you collected contact information and set up communication channels so you (and your partner and children, if applicable) can stay in touch with friends and family?

- Are you clear about what needs to be packed, what will fit in your new accommodation, what needs to be shipped quickly or otherwise, and what must absolutely travel with you?

- Have you planned to take care of yourself (and other family members, if applicable) as you experience the physical and emotional demands of the move?

# 9

## SETTLING IN

*"This is the bright home*
*in which I live,*
*this is where*
*I ask*
*my friends*
*to come,*
*this is where I want*
*to love all the things*
*it has taken me so long*
*to learn to love."*

**David Whyte,** *The House of Belonging (excerpt)*

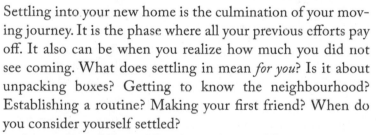

Settling into your new home is the culmination of your moving journey. It is the phase where all your previous efforts pay off. It also can be when you realize how much you did not see coming. What does settling in mean *for you*? Is it about unpacking boxes? Getting to know the neighbourhood? Establishing a routine? Making your first friend? When do you consider yourself settled?

Jenny moved from New York City to The Hague with her husband, Jared, and their daughter, Sonia. Prior to the move, she was working as a legal counsel for a media company and her husband was a human rights lawyer with the United Nations. He got an offer to work at the International Criminal Court (ICC), and they moved to the Netherlands when Sonia was ten years old. Jared moved in late spring and his wife and daughter followed as soon as schools closed for the summer vacation.

They were both working full time before the move, so they did not have much time to prepare. Jenny quit her job, but had to work through her notice period, which ended only a couple of weeks before the move. They decided to keep their furniture and appliances in storage in the US and ship only clothes and kitchenware to the Netherlands. When Jared arrived, he found an apartment and negotiated with the previous renters to buy some of their furniture, including beds, a dining table and chairs. He quickly ordered a sofa, a couple of desks and some lamps, and had them assembled before his family arrived.

Jenny and Jared did not know anyone in The Hague, but before they left, a good friend from New York put them in touch with his friend Steve, who had lived there for several years. Steve was Jared's lifeline in the first few weeks. Together they toured different neighbourhoods until Jared found suitable accommodation. Steve helped him set up basic services for their new apartment, introduced him to the new neighbourhood and, when it was time, welcomed the family to The Hague.

They passed the first few months in a fog. Jenny spent most of her time getting Sonia settled at home and school, getting to know her way around and starting to learn Dutch. The family mostly spent the weekends with Steve, his wife Dana, and their kids, who were 9 and 11.

Sonia's transition to her new life was not smooth. Besides struggling with the language, she also did not want to spend any time in her new room. In order to save her daughter the trouble (and to be able to discard unnecessary toys without objections), Jenny had both packed and unpacked Sonia's moving boxes, so she did not have anything to do with what her new room looked like.

Just seven months after Jenny and Jared had arrived, Steve and Dana moved back to the US. Their departure left Jenny feeling very alone. Besides Steve and his family, she had not made friends in their new city. She was in regular contact with family and close friends back in New York City, but that was it: her social life revolved around video calls. She fell into a depression that lasted almost a year.

Jenny and Jared's story points out some common mistakes that expats – especially those on their first international move – make when settling into a new place. They add to the already high stresses of the move, delay everyone's adjustment and can even negatively affect the assignee's performance at work. Here are some key traps to avoid.

## COMMON MISTAKES

1. **Not thinking about creating home.** In the rush to get themselves and their families settled in, many expats fail to consider what their new dwellings should provide – such as familiarity and connection to their past life, a safe haven for their children and/or a comfortable workspace. These considerations should have been the starting point. Jenny and Jared did not consider this and, as a result, ended up with a mishmash of furniture they 'inherited' or did not choose jointly and a room their daughter didn't enjoy.

2. **Not building a broad base of support.** Getting caught up in the frenzy of settling in can create the illusion that there is no time to socialize. Expats end up isolating themselves that way and may not realize it until several months into their new life, like Jenny did. Without the invaluable practical and emotional support a network can provide, adjustment just takes longer. Jenny spent too much time on video calls and not enough time getting out of the apartment and talking to people locally.

3. **Not anticipating the stages of adjustment.** With all that is going on, it's easy to forget that post-move adjustment experiences can differ significantly among family members. Anchored in his new job, with a built-in support system, Jared adjusted quickly. Jenny did not pay attention to the initial symptoms of depression. When she did not

have the energy to get out of bed in the mornings, she thought it was because of the darkness outside and her body adjusting to the Dutch winter. It took her several months of suffering before she sought professional help.

## HOW TO SETTLE IN AFTER A MOVE

Settling into a new place is the phase where all the core principles discussed in the first part of the book – the importance of home, personality, family and the stages of adjustment – come together to shape the experience of expatriation. Organized around these principles, this chapter shows you how to apply them to settle in and thrive in your new life. Ideally, you will have laid the foundations in the preparation and moving phases. But even if you have not, it's not too late to take action. Here's how.

### Focus First on the Familiar

Settling in is all about creating a new home, so make it a priority. By now, you should have asked yourself (and your partner/family) essential questions, discussed in Chapter 1, including "What is home?" and "What do I/we need to do to create home?" and done some preparatory work. Now, it is time to focus on the practical, emotional and social aspects of creating home. As you do this, keep in mind differences in family members' concepts of home and needs for support.

#### Unpack and arrange your home ASAP

If you have favourite objects or items that will immediately add a homey touch to your new place, unpack those first. For most expats, this will be photos of family and friends, but kitchenware, candles, books and favourite paintings also give a feeling of home. Hopefully, you will have packed those items separately during the moving phase.

Think of what relaxes or energizes you, and arrange and decorate your space accordingly. If you need a space to read, create a cosy reading area with a comfortable chair or a sofa and pillows. Do you need a corner for special projects or hobbies, such as sewing or painting, or one for playing board games? If you like to entertain, what would you like your entertaining space to look like? While space limitations and financial considerations are legitimate, making a place feel like home does not necessarily take a lot of space or money.

## Help your children set up their rooms

Make it a priority to unpack their boxes with them and help them get settled in their rooms. Give your children control over how to structure and decorate their new rooms, but make sure to include familiar objects, such as toys, books or bedding. One of the first things our daughter does is hang up posters of her favourite football players. Every time David moved as a child, setting up his room was his top priority, and he had a specific set of rituals for doing that: "It had to have a comfortable bed, a reading corner, my favourite pictures on the walls, somewhere I could play my favourite music. I couldn't control the fact that we moved, but I *could* control how I set up my room, and that made me feel grounded and secure in the midst of so much change."

## Strive to maintain familiar routines

Sustaining small habits can be as helpful as picking up new ones in reinforcing and speeding up adjustment. One of the first things Nina, a Danish expat, does when she moves to a new place is join a gym and volunteer at a cat shelter. That way she can connect with people who have similar interests. Find a café you like, a restaurant, a food store, an outdoor market and become a regular. It's a great way to create a sense of home, but also to meet new people – the owners, employees or other regulars.

A settled family routine minimizes disruption in your children's lives. Strive to keep the same schedule for meals and bedtime, household responsibilities and family celebrations, among others. Maintain family rituals, whether it's pizza-and-movie night, elaborate weekend breakfasts or family bike rides, to provide continuity and a sense of home.

**Sign up for favourite activities**
Whether it's continuing a hobby, learning the local language or a new skill, immediately establishing new routines helps you put structure to your days (especially if you are not working at the moment) and make social connections at the same time.

Picking up familiar activities, such as a favourite sport, will also help your children feel more connected. If you did your planning and have some options lined up for them already when you get there, all the better. Otherwise, try to establish new routines as soon as possible. Use the resources described in Chapter 7 on planning and preparation.

Find a unique 'hook' for each child – some activity or routine that will allow them to integrate and feel at home faster. Team sports, for example, are a great 'integrator'. Being part of the local football club helped our children meet new friends and build confidence. For another child, it may be joining the school's drama club.

## Start the Adjustment Process
Even as you seek to retain the familiar, you should judiciously begin the adjustment process. The earlier you start to do this, the better.

**Explore your neighbourhood**
Find out the 'basics', such as how to get to work and to the children's school, and where the closest supermarket, shopping area, restaurants, cafés or other 'necessities' are located. Go out, walk around, take public transport, visit museums and shops.

Talk to people – your neighbours, the mothers at the play-ground, the family sitting next to you at the local coffee shop. Immerse yourself in the culture. Be curious and interested.

If you have children, take them with you. Look at maps and find your way around together. Sylvia, a South African woman who followed her husband to Berlin, did exactly that: "Not staying home, even if we did not know where we were going and did not even have a map, was important. It showed my kids that you can end up anywhere in the world and, as long as you go out and embrace it, you can make whatever you want out of it." If school has not started yet, take advantage of the free time to figure out distances and itineraries, especially if some of your children will be going to school by themselves.

**Sample local food**
Incorporate local cuisine into your life. Besides enriching your experience of the culture, using local ingredients is more accessible and usually cheaper than trying to get foreign products to recreate your home cuisine. Sabine and Alex's son had to get used to eating Chinese noodles in Singapore, rather than his favourite, but now very expensive, imported Italian pasta.

That said, there will also be times when you will crave the comfort of familiar food, especially in the beginning, or if you have children. Whenever Christian, an Austrian expat, moves to a new country, one of the first things he does to feel settled is to "try to get food from home to have a hearty welcome dinner. Even if it is just a Milka chocolate bar." Locating a store with food from your home country, if available, will allow you to get that little piece of home when you need it.

**Find a cultural mentor**
This can be a neighbour, work colleague or another parent from the school. It can be a friend of a friend, an experienced expat who has been through the adaptation process already

or a local you were introduced to. It should be someone you feel comfortable with. When Abigail, an American, and her family first moved to Vienna, they knew nothing about living in Austria. "Most of my support came from another mother I met at the American School, where our children went. They had moved to Vienna a few years earlier, so she'd been there and helped me figure out a lot of things. She was my piece of home. I knew I could always call her if I needed anything. That was huge."

### Organize some cultural orientation

Use the internet, social media and local listings (e.g., the local tourist board) to look up events taking place in your area. Whether it's concerts, museums, local traditions or other fun events and sights around town, make a list of places you want to go and immerse yourself in the local culture.

Getting to know the culture is another area where you can build on the work you did in the preparation phase. But even if you haven't done much, take advantage now of being immersed in the culture. Talk to people, but also listen to what they talk about, observe how they talk, the gestures they make, the jokes they laugh at. When I move to a new place, I like to read books about my new home, especially fiction, which gives me a different picture of the 'soul' of the culture than a guidebook would. When I moved to Paris, I started with Julia Child's *My Life in France*, Ernest Hemingway's *A Moveable Feast* and Adam Gopnik's *Paris to the Moon*.

Learning about a place is an ongoing process. Keep being curious, observing and asking questions. If you started language lessons before the move, keep learning. It will be easier since you will be immersed. If you haven't, get language lessons for you and your family immediately upon arrival.

## Build Your Support Network

When you move abroad, you leave behind your network of supportive relationships. Ideally, you will already have done some preparatory work for setting up your new network. Regardless, you need to give it priority and real commitment. Think of what you need to feel supported. Is it an emergency contact? A sympathetic ear when you're struggling with adjustment? Someone who shares your professional or personal interests (for instance, a writers' circle)? Staying in touch with the people you leave behind is as important as making new connections. Both sets of relationships, new and old, will provide support that can improve your transition and that of your family. Here are some ways to build and maintain those relationships.

### Find your new tribe

Friends won't just show up at your doorstep. Be proactive about making new connections. Sylvia, the South African I mentioned earlier, did exactly that. "I got out of the apartment right away, wandering around Berlin and talking to people. My closest friend here I met at the subway station when I asked her for directions on our second day in Berlin."

Think of the natural places to meet people, depending on your lifestyle: the workplace, the children's school, the local gym. Join a sports club, the local expat organization, the parent-teacher association or other parent group, the neighbourhood association. If you are lucky enough to know someone local already, great; but make a point of going out and meeting more new people.

Seasoned expats know that, in the beginning, you need to say yes to every invitation you get, whether you are really interested or not. Also, even if you don't get invited, be proactive about suggesting meetings with people you meet. That may mean you will have to get out of your comfort zone. For example, if the local culture permits it, go ring the doorbell of your new neighbours and invite them for drinks at your house. The more people you interact with, the likelier that you will find among them your future best friends. Don't hesitate to offer help; sometimes a small amount of effort on your part can have a significant benefit for the other and help cement a new relationship.

If your children go to an international school, most other parents there are likely to be in similar situations as yours, which should help you build connection fast. If you don't have children, or if your children are not school-age yet, joining sports or other interest-based clubs, learning a new skill or taking language lessons are solid avenues for meeting new people, especially if you want to reach beyond the expat community.

Whether it is through shared passions (e.g., a gourmet cooking group) or hobbies (a photography club), professional interests (a writers' circle), sports (a runners' club) or other common elements (English-speaking parents in Paris), joining a community of like-minded people is a great way to build new friendships. If you are an expat partner, most locations have expat partner support networks. It's relatively simple to find opportunities for connection by searching online, but make sure the goal is eventually to arrange face-to-face meetings with your virtual connections. Create habits and routines with your new friends. Friendships are easier to maintain if they are linked by some kind of regular common practice, such as a weekly coffee meeting or monthly book club. If you cannot find a group corresponding to your interests in your location, start one! Fiona is an Irish writer, married to a Dutch diplomat. Wherever they've moved, she has searched for a writers' circle to join. When she could not find one in Manila, she started her own, with great success.

If local connections are your goal, be persistent. Friendships with locals may be harder to establish than those with other expats, but tend to last longer (not least because locals don't move!) and can make you feel more grounded and integrated.

If it's taking you a long time to make friends, don't become disappointed or depressed. Building connections takes time and the process is different for every person. For instance, when I move to a new place, I know from experience that it will take me at least a year, usually longer, to form a small circle of friends. For my massively extroverted friend, Philip, a couple months are enough.

Finding a new tribe every time we move takes time, effort and commitment. For expats, this tribe becomes our substitute family, the people who care for and support us, who have fun with us, but who also are there for us in difficult times and in emergencies.

### Help your children get connected

Every time they move, your children will have to rebuild their circle of friends. Some (older children, extroverts, experienced movers) will find that easier than others, but most will need your help to get started.

Start with the school environment. Whether your child is in preschool or high school, schedule a meeting with their teacher(s) before school starts. Give them some background on your child: their likes and dislikes, strengths and weak spots, anything you think will help the teacher understand where your child is coming from and make them feel comfortable in their new class. Especially if your child does not go to an international school (where teachers are used to dealing with new arrivals), make sure the teacher understands the parameters of your child's transition, and the potential practical and emotional challenges (schooling in a different language than before, the need to make new friends). Don't hesitate to ask for something that you know would help your child feel more comfortable. Carla asked her son's new third grade teacher in Atlanta whether it would be possible to assign another student as his 'buddy' for the first couple of months. That buddy, a fourth grader, helped Marco navigate the new school system, but also made sure that he did not feel completely isolated and lost as the new kid at school.

At least for the first few months of school, agree that you will check in with the teachers on a regular basis to monitor your child's adjustment, in terms of academic performance, but especially social integration. When our children started school in Zurich, we agreed with their teachers that if either of us noticed any unusual behaviour (such as being withdrawn, aggressive or otherwise visibly distressed) or felt that something was 'off', we would contact each other. Having an open line of communication helps you catch potential problems early on.

Get to know other parents. If you have time, join the parent's association or volunteer for other school activities. Especially if your child is in the first years of primary school, it's a great way of keeping an eye on them while getting to know other parents.

You can't make friends for your child, but you can create opportunities for them to do so themselves. Organize play dates, especially if your child is younger. Be creative. A mother I know packed little bags of candy and had her son bring them to his classmates on his first day of class, as a get-to-know-you gift. Each bag had a tag on it with her phone number, encouraging other parents to call and schedule a play date. She immediately heard back from a few other parents. Play dates can really make a difference in speeding up your child's integration at school. They get to know other children better and you may also be able to get to know their parents and perhaps make new friends. It's a win-win.

Also, support your child in making local friends outside of school. Participating in extracurricular activities can help with your child's adjustment. If your child goes to a local school, their classmates will live nearby. This is not necessarily so for an international school. Get in touch with other families in your neighbourhood and organize get-togethers. Local friends will help them feel more connected and will give them something to do on the weekends. Don't talk about how long you will be staying. If you are there on a limited assignment, unfortunately there are people – even children! – who will be put off by that fact and may not be interested in getting to know you or your children.

If you have a pre-teen or teenager, make sure they are comfortable with your level of involvement in their school life. They may not want you hovering around the school or running for president of the parent-teacher association from day one. It may be easier for them to adjust and feel independent if you're *not* around all the time.

Finally, be careful about how much pressure you put on your child during those early weeks of adjustment. They already are coping with navigating an unfamiliar environment, potentially a new language and fitting into a new class. They don't need you breathing down their neck about their grades. Also, I highly recommend to wait and see how they handle the school workload before you push them to take advanced classes or fill their calendar with extracurricular activities.

## Nurture your existing network

Connection with family and friends back home is a lifesaver during those lonely first few weeks or months. Creating and maintaining that connection takes real commitment and planning. Call, email, remember birthdays and milestones, actively show interest, share what's going on in your world and make an effort to keep up with what's going on in theirs (for example, through social media or chat groups). Make a list of the people who are important to you and schedule the first few catch-up calls with them. Establish a routine and manage expectations for how often you will be in touch. Even if you have to put a reminder on your phone or calendar, connect with your loved ones at least once every two weeks. As the one who leaves, you should take the initiative keeping in touch, sharing news, and asking for and offering support.

While modern technology has made it easier to stay in touch, it cannot replace real-time relationships. Encourage your loved ones to visit (and be prepared that some locations may prove more popular than others). Also, try to visit friends and family as much as is realistic. Going back home or to a place where you've lived can be a complex organizational and scheduling challenge, but it is worth it, especially for children. Organizing joint vacations with friends and family is another way to stay in touch.

For children, the need for contact with family and friends back home is even more intense. Especially if they are school-age or older, they will most likely be unhappy about leaving behind their loved ones. Provide them with support and resources to stay in touch. Especially for teenagers, close friends are a valuable source of support when they go through transition. I try to balance my parental urge to limit their time on social media with the knowledge that these platforms can be a lifeline in terms of allowing them to stay connected with their friends.

## Do What You Can to Ease the Transition

In Chapter 2, we discussed the stages of transition – honeymoon, crisis, recovery and adjustment – for those who want to move, and also the stages of grieving for those who don't. Even if this is not your first move, understanding where you are at in the transition can ease the process of adjustment. It helps to know what comes when, what is ahead, what you can look forward to and what you should look out for.

**Recognize where you are**

Be alert to the physical and emotional symptoms of each stage. If you notice your spirits shifting from excitement to frustration and a sense of feeling overwhelmed, maybe you have moved from honeymoon to crisis. If you find yourself feeling more competent and able to function in your new environment, maybe you're in recovery or even approaching adjustment. Anticipate challenges and get appropriate support, but also be encouraged by the fact that these symptoms, just as the stages they represent, are transient. Knowing that there is a curve and having a sense of what part of the curve you are on helps you look forward to the next stage.

If you are moving with a partner or family, be mindful that their transition experience will most likely differ from yours, as will the stage they are in at any given point. Everyone experiences change differently. As the assignee, the new job will be an anchor and you likely will be familiar with your company culture and may already know some colleagues. Your partner and children are likely to feel much greater culture shock and/or experience more isolation. They also will probably carry a heavier logistical burden.

To cope better with the different stages of transition, stay connected with yourself, your partner and your family. Even if you're extremely busy at work, it is critical to remember to do the following.

**Engage in self-care**
Take into account your personality type. If you are introverted, make sure you give yourself downtime and space to recharge when you need to. If you are uncomfortable with change, and not so comfortable with new experiences or if you tend to see things negatively, you may be more prone to the stress of relocation, so find outlets (sports, creative hobbies, socializing) to get rid of emotional and physical tension. If you need a secure base to retreat to when you get overwhelmed (e.g., a home or room filled with familiar and comforting objects), then make creating that base a priority.

When Kate and Jonathan's son, Adam, would get homesick in their new home in London, "We would get him mac and cheese from the box, which we would find at a little American grocery store." Find whatever it is that helps you manage homesickness – from home food to phone calls with your loved ones to regular trips home – and indulge when you need to.

Don't try to do it all alone. Allow yourself to grieve and experience loss, but if at some point you find yourself over-whelmed, anxious or even depressed, don't hesitate to seek help. Being homesick or down does not make you a failure. Give yourself a break. Call a friend and vent. That's one of the reasons why nurturing your existing network is critical. If things get rough, a mental health professional should be able to help you get perspective and cope better.

Give yourself permission, too, to slow down. Even the simplest tasks are likely to take much longer in the begin-ning, so expect that and don't put yourself under pressure to function like you did in your previous location.

There will be times when, especially if you are a first-time expat, you will get impatient. You may think: "It's been a year already, why do I still not feel like I fit in?" or "Why do I have so few friends after six months?" Building a new life takes time. You will make mistakes. You will start over. You will learn to do things a different way. You will rebuild your con-fidence, your relationship with your partner, your connection with your children. In the end, you will find your own balance and sense of home. Appreciate what you've already achieved. Pause regularly and get some perspective.

**Expect surprises**

We already discussed in Chapter 2 how the transition process is non-linear and different for every person. Temper expec-tations for how it should go, keep an open mind and always check your assumptions.

You may think that you know a place because you've trav-elled there before. Tourism is not real life; business travel is even less so. Once you settle somewhere, what you thought was interesting or cute or exotic becomes your daily reality –

minus the excitement of novelty. Things may now bother you that didn't previously because you were just visiting and now have to deal with them on a regular basis. Also, though you may think you know and understand the culture of the place you are moving to, that does not mean that you will adjust instantly. Just because you have watched Hollywood movies doesn't mean that you know American culture. Finally, don't think that you know a culture because you speak the language. Language, although important, does not define culture; culture defines culture. Ask French-Canadians moving to Belgium, or Americans moving to Australia.

It's going to take time, so be measured in your expectations on how easily you will fit in. Strive to be curious and interested in learning. Accept the differences and resist the temptation to make comparisons with your previous home. Critically, understand how your own culture has influenced you, but also how it affects the way others see you. Every culture has stereotypes that follow it to other countries and what people see in you may sometimes have more to do with the country that you are from, than with who you really are. Just be aware of that.

Finally, don't expect that experience with previous moves makes you immune from culture shock and the adjustment process. Every move is unique because every country, culture and society are different and present distinct challenges. You may have made a lot of mistakes – and learned from them – but there are plenty more out there to be made and learned from. Manage your expectations and be prepared to do the work.

### Keep nurturing your relationship

Take the time to create some couple rituals. Maybe you have some already that you can re-create – a weekly date night or game of tennis, or the occasional weekend away. Maybe there are new rituals you want to try out – like the yoga studio in your neighbourhood.

Schedule regular quality time together. If you no longer have family around to babysit, and if your partner travels during the week, be creative to find ways to do that. Focus on things you both love – a sport, a visit to a museum, a concert – then decompress and enjoy each other's company. Be intentional and consistent in planning, booking dates in your calendars and then actually following through. Find ways to connect that you can pursue consistently, daily, weekly and monthly. While finding the time may be challenging when starting a new job, your availability during the first few weeks of the move will be crucial both for getting everyone off to a good start and for the health of your relationships with your partner and family.

Make a point of knowing what's going on in your partner's world at any given time, *especially* if your experiences are very different. Reach out, rather than expecting them to do that.

Show your appreciation on a daily basis, especially if your partner made career (or other) sacrifices to move with you. Be alert that they could go through a range of not-so-positive emotions, including anger, regret, frustration or outright distress. Understand what matters to them and what they need in order to adjust to their new life, so you can support them as best you can.

Anna, the Dutch woman who moved to her husband's hometown in Slovenia, emphasizes how much it meant to her that he understood her frustrations. "He had also lived abroad before we met, so he had gone through similar challenges. I would have found it very hard to adjust if he hadn't had empathy for what I was going through." Her husband's readiness to step in and help her out, for instance in dealing with bureaucratic matters, also made a difference. "He understands that, although I speak the language, I am not completely comfortable. He knows how difficult it is and I appreciate that."

If you partner handled most of the logistics of the move, acknowledge their contribution and express your appreciation. Their efforts and support have been instrumental in your being able to carry on with your work.

If your partner is the one being relocated and you are not working (or not yet), setting up a routine provides structure to your day, gives you something to look forward to and helps you have a sense of purpose and achievement.

**Prioritize connecting with your children**
Every child copes with moving and adjustment in their own way. Anticipate how your child is likely to deal with the move, so that you can support them as best you can. But be prepared for surprises. The child you expect to breeze through the move may have the most difficulty, while the one you think will struggle may do relatively well. Here's how you can support your children through the adjustment process and help them feel at home in their new environment.

Start by educating them about transition. Most kids have no idea how it works, so show them a picture of the adjustment curve. Talk about the different points on the curve. Reassure them that most people, including their parents, go through the same stages and challenges, but also that almost everyone ends up in a good place at the top of the curve – at home.

Besides helping them understand that how they feel is perfectly normal, and that they are not the only ones going through it, express your confidence in their ability to manage the process and come out on the other side. This will encourage them to see relocation challenges as both temporary and within their power to overcome. Cheer for them, but be careful not to add your expectations to their list of challenges.

## Help Your Children Build Resilience
Children who go through transitions successfully develop confidence and skills for life. They learn to make new friends,

integrate in a new environment and become comfortable with change. They develop the ability to tackle and overcome adversity, a skill known as resilience. Here's how you can support them in building up that resilience.

### Adopt a growth mindset

Child psychologist Kate Berger talks about cultivating a growth mindset[1] – the belief that their most basic abilities can be developed through dedication and hard work, not just brains and talent. By encouraging children to see difficulties as challenges that can be overcome, you show that you believe in them and help them develop confidence in their own abilities and resourcefulness. Ask them to think of different ways to tackle a problem. Compliment them when they handle a situation well. Allow them to make mistakes, but be there to help them learn from those and bounce back.

### Educate them about family history

Studies show that the more children know about their family's history, the more they feel that they are part of a larger whole, have a sense of control over their lives and are more resilient when faced with stress. A strong family narrative, especially one about family members facing challenges, overcoming them successfully and moving on, tends to be associated with higher self-esteem, better emotional health and happiness.[2]

How can you convey a sense of family history as a parent? Tell family stories, both yours and those of your ancestors. Maintain family traditions and rituals, whether it is special occasions, such as family vacations and holidays or simple daily routines. Especially if you move regularly, keep records – journals, photos, postcards or other souvenirs – of special places you go or things you do together as a family. Your children will want to have a record of those experiences, as they are part of who they are.

As we saw in Chapter 4, children have a wide range of reactions and need different kinds of support depending on their age, stage of development and personality. If you move with an infant or toddler, they will not notice much. A pre-schooler might have a vague idea what's going on, but a move is unlikely to have a lasting emotional impact. The most you need to do to help them feel comfortable is maintain their routines and surround them with some familiar objects. Your presence is, of course, a key prerequisite for them to feel safe and secure. Even if you have already organized childcare in your new home, try to be around your children as much as possible.

The older your children are, the more actively you will need to support them. While the teenage years are the worst time to relocate, sometimes that is unavoidable. Below are some ways to help your school-age child, pre-teen or teenager cope with transition.

1. **Make time** to be with them on a daily basis. Be present and available physically, but also emotionally.
2. **Observe.** Check on them regularly. The signs that something is wrong vary for each child: some become quiet and withdrawn, while others are irritable, aggressive and disruptive. Their behaviour may be different at school than at home. If you see symptoms that make you uncomfortable, consider consulting with a specialist.
3. **Listen.** Keep the lines of communication open. Ask them what they need from you to feel supported through the move. Encourage them to talk about their impressions of their new home, the school, the other children, their expectations and their feelings. What is it that worries them the most? What do they look forward to? Make addressing their concerns a priority.

During the first six months of their new life in The Hague, Jenny's daughter, Sonia, normally a quiet, cooperative child, became defiant and confrontational, especially towards her mother. Concerned by this sudden change, Jenny and Jared asked for help from the school psychologist, who told them that this was most likely a reaction to the move, and that it would get better as Sonia became more settled. Then one evening, as Jenny was kissing her daughter goodnight, the subject of the move came up, and Sonia revealed that she was mad at her mother for making the move.

"But it was your father's job that brought us here," Jenny protested.

"Yes, but you agreed to move," Sonia replied.

Jenny would have never thought this was the reason her daughter was being so difficult. The family sat down and had a long talk about the move and why they had decided to go for it. After that, Sonia's behaviour improved dramatically.

Judiciously try to get your children to talk about their losses and how they feel about them. What are they missing the most? Friends and family, places, routines? Help them articulate what they are feeling and show that you are really listening. Even if they don't answer or become irritated when you ask, they know that you are there and ready to help. Many expat children feel like they don't have permission to feel sad, because they lead privileged lives compared to their peers. By letting them talk about their losses, you recognize and validate them. Give them permission and time to grieve. If you always try to cheer them up, by insisting that "it will pass" or that "it's nothing serious" and they should "look at the bright side," it may sound like you are discounting their loss.

Understand, and help them to understand, that it will take time – anything from six months to a year, maybe more – until they feel settled. Be prepared for strong reactions and do your best. There will be ups and downs, excitement and anger, sadness and anxiety, but in the end, they will find their balance.

Be real about your own emotions and how you are coping with the transition. Model behaviour and your children will follow suit. If they see you making an effort, being open and interested, embracing your new life, and handling the stresses of the move with humour and resilience, they will feel encouraged to do the same.

At the same time, try to keep a balance between maintaining a positive attitude and being honest. Struggling with depression, feeling overwhelmed and isolated, Jenny did not want her daughter to know how difficult she was finding their transition to life in the Netherlands. Sonia sensed that something was wrong, however, and perceived it as her mother not being honest. This made her distress even more intense. Culture shock can affect everyone. Knowing that their parents are not immune will help normalize the experience for your children.

Even if they seem to be coping well, keep an eye on them for signs of distress, such as significant weight loss or gain, mood changes, fatigue or sudden drops in performance at school, among others. Sometimes it's hard to tell those symptoms from the normal consequences of developmental changes (for instance, mood swings in teenagers), but it's better to be alert than to be late in getting them support.

Be prepared to ask for professional help, even if it seems early in the process. Some children may be struggling even before the move takes place. Ideally, have some contacts lined up already before the move. Also, be aware that your child's reaction can be time-delayed. Many expat parents wait too long to ask for help, when their children (and the family in general) would have benefited from earlier support.

## Have a 'Plan B'

Be sure to give some serious thought to what happens if things don't work out as planned or if adversity strikes: you lose your job, your relationship or marriage breaks down, your partner gets injured or dies, among others. Some potential disasters are location-specific: for example, some areas have a higher likelihood of natural disasters (earthquakes, hurricanes) or political unrest (coups, civil unrest) happening. Emergency plans are necessary in our home countries, but doubly so in a foreign land. Besides having the emergency numbers pinned on your fridge at home and an emergency contact lined up, it is important to:

a) have a clear idea what could go wrong; and

b) have plans for coping, should that happen.

What are your worst-case scenarios? What would you need to protect yourself and your family in any of those cases? Here are some thoughts.

Find out about your legal rights in your new country, in particular the legal framework around matters that could affect you. For instance, if you are moving with your spouse and children, even if there's nothing wrong with your marriage, look into your respective rights in case of separation or divorce, or the laws governing the custody of children. Recognize that these will likely be different than the ones in your home country. When Lily's husband announced that he was leaving her, quitting his position and moving back to his home country, the Netherlands, they were one year into his foreign assignment in Addis Ababa. Before she could recover from the emotional shock, Lily, with no job or funds of her own, had to move out of their home and take the kids out of private school – both paid by her husband's employer – while figuring out where to go next.

If you are financially dependent on your partner, either from before the current move or because of it, find out what happens in the following scenarios, if relevant:

1. If your right to remain in the country (visa or residence permit) is linked to your partner, what happens if they get fired or decide to separate from you?

2. If you and your partner have joint assets, including bank accounts, what happens if one of you dies or is incapacitated? Do you still have access and the right to manage them?
3. What happens to custody of your children in case you or your partner die or you separate?
4. If you have a will, living will or power of attorney, are these valid and enforceable in your country of residence if something happens to either or both of you? Seek an attorney who specializes in international legal issues to find out for you. Then plan accordingly. If you can't find a legal expert in the country you're in, seek one in your home country.

These are only some of the questions you should be asking yourself. Find ways to protect yourself and your family in case any of those scenarios materializes. For example, it's always a good idea to maintain a personal bank account in your name, wherever you live. If that's not possible in your host country because you don't earn your own income, then at least don't get rid of any accounts you have in your home country. Make sure you have a legal advisor lined up, just in case. This may all sound extreme, but expat horror stories are common, so don't put yourself in a vulnerable position.

## Take Control of Your Life

Finally, you cannot control a lot of the parameters of relocation, but you can control your intention – the goals you set for yourself and what gives meaning to your life. Emilia, the Hungarian expat we met in a previous chapter, resolved that, even though her husband leads their relocations, she sees herself as a manager of her own destiny, not as a follower. A child psychologist, she decided to build a portable career, catering to expat children and offering counselling in person but also remotely, through video calls. "You need to focus on your own objectives and your own career. It's very tempting to get into the excuse and blaming mode. Get in the driver's seat, even if sometimes you feel that you don't really have control over your life. You always have choices, and you are always leading."

If you are planning on getting back to work, go to networking events in your field. This is easier if you have done your homework in the planning phase. If not, talk to people, do online research, especially check out Meetups, professional associations or other organizations in your field. Have a clear intention for those events: what do you want to get out of them? Put yourself out there, be genuinely curious, make connections and follow up.

Whether it's journal writing, reading, music (playing or listening), dancing, writing poetry, painting, other forms of creative expression, or physical activities such as sports or other hobbies, taking the time to do something for yourself will benefit your soul and give you the energy to keep going. Kate, the diplomatic spouse, decided to create a space where she could develop herself. "I needed something just for me. My frustration made me think about what I could do to feel better and the answer was to find an identity that does not have anything to do with my children or my husband. I needed something that would be unrelated to my role as a parent, wife or representative of my country in a foreign land." Kate joined an online forum of people who were interested in theatre, anonymously at first. "There were a lot of people there who were creative writers, so that got me started on writing, as well. That really saved my sanity and the writing is something I kept up when we moved back to the States."

Settling in may be the end of your expat move, but it is only the beginning of your expat journey. There will be challenges. There will be triumphs. You will feel exhilarated, and you will feel exasperated. And then one day you will wake up, look out the window and realize that there's no place you'd rather be.

# CHECKLIST

- What is your plan for creating home in your new residence as soon as possible? What can you do to help your children feel at home in their new rooms? What family rituals will you prioritize continuing?

- How will you and your family begin the process of learning about and engaging with your new location and its culture?

- How will you educate your partner and children about the process of transition and help support them through it?

- What is your plan for building your new support network? For supporting your partner and children in building theirs?

- Do you have a 'Plan B'? What are the potential contingencies you need to anticipate and be ready to deal with?

# 10

MOVING AS A
SINGLE EXPAT

*"Don't be scared to walk alone*
*Don't be scared to like it."*

**John Mayer,** *"The Age of Worry" (lyrics)*

More people than ever before are single – and the numbers
are growing. According to data from the US Census Bureau,
110.6 million people, or over 45% of all US residents 18 or
older, were single in 2016 as compared to 28% in 1970.[1]
Similar trends in many other countries make singles the fast-
est-growing household group in most parts of the world.[2]

This trend is reflected in expatriation, as more single
expats move abroad and more married expats choose to take
assignments without their partners or families. According to
the annual relocation trends survey by BGRS, single men and
women constituted almost a third (32%) of the total number of expat assignees surveyed in 2016. That number was
up by 6% from 2015. In addition to increasing numbers of
single expat assignees, the proportion of partnered or married assignees who, for a variety of reasons, choose to go on
long-term assignments as 'single-status' (i.e., without their
partners), also has been increasing – from 20% in 2015 to
27% in 2016.[3]

There are many positives to being a single expat. A key
advantage is freedom and flexibility, which brings with it
excitement and a sense of adventure. Many of the single expats
I interviewed consider the opportunity to reinvent themselves
as one of the best parts about their new lives. This is expressed
in statements such as, "As a single expat, you are light."

"You start with a clean slate every time. Everything is possible." "You make your own choices." "You are free to do whatever you like, when you like to." The situation of single-status expats is different, but still has significant positive aspects. Those that I interviewed, said things like, "I don't have to worry about my family and can focus on work," "Neither I nor my partner have to compromise our careers" and "We wanted the career opportunity without the total life overhaul."

When travelling and/or living abroad on your own, you can gain a deeper knowledge of yourself, especially an awareness of capabilities you did not know you had. Research shows that moving as a single makes you more self-sufficient, confident and resilient. You get used to coping on your own. When new challenges appear, you know that you can handle them.

Finally, as a single expat you have the time, space and energy to focus on your own development, whether it is professional development and building your career, or tending to your personal growth and wellbeing. You have no one else to take care of but yourself. This also allows you the time and motivation to nurture your relationships – old and new – which is an added advantage, but also an essential element of single expat life.

Still, moving as a single poses its own challenges.

Susan left her home in the US Midwest to move to Tokyo with little preparation. "No one else from my family had ever lived abroad. I had no idea, no guidance on what it meant to be an expat. The only thing I did was decide I was going, and then spend a year saving money. I went skydiving that year. If I could jump out of a plane, I could do anything," Susan explains. Another skydiver brought a massive coffee-table book on Tokyo to show Susan, but she couldn't look at it. "If I looked at the pictures, I would never take the leap." When Susan arrived at Tokyo's Narita Airport, she was shocked to discover that all the signs were in Japanese. And she'd never ridden a train before. "I stood with my luggage after a 24-hour flight with no idea how to get to the place where I was supposed to be staying."

While deciding to move is more straightforward for singles, preparation – or more precisely the lack thereof – was a recurring theme in my interviews. People moving alone often think they will not have many challenges, because they only have themselves to think of. A modest amount of advance planning would have saved Susan months of confusion, as she tried to figure out and navigate the new culture.

## WHAT TO FOCUS ON WHEN MOVING ALONE

Like people moving with a partner or family, single expats need to make an informed decision, plan thoroughly, organize and execute their move, and settle into their new environment. Much of what has already been written in this book is valid for single expat moves, such as the need to define one's intention, consider long-term goals, think through the implications of a move before deciding and engage in self-care during stressful times.

However, single expats face some unique challenges and have different priorities compared to someone moving with a partner or family. Most obviously, they lack the practical and emotional support that a partner or spouse can provide. They are more vulnerable to loneliness. They are more prone to stretching themselves thin, as they try to balance work (especially the tendency to work long hours) and the process of moving and settling in all by themselves. Finally, the single expats' social life, both past and present, tends to be both their highest priority and their biggest challenge.

Single expats will find much helpful information that applies to them in all previous chapters of this book. This chapter will look at each phase of a move, highlight challenges that are unique for single expats, and point out priorities and steps for speeding up adjustment and making the most of that move.

## WHEN DECIDING

Decision-making seems simple and straightforward when there is only one decision maker and one set of parameters. You run the show, you are only responsible for yourself and do not need to compromise for someone else's needs or wants. At the same time, the weight of the decision, and its consequences, fall entirely on you. That said, you can turn to many different people for advice. When Susan moved to Tokyo, she only had support from a friend of a friend's brother who'd been to Japan and her local parish priest, who gave her the address of a Jesuit mission in Tokyo as a place to land. "After that, I learned my lesson. When I moved to a new country, I gathered support and advice from friends, my sister, other expats, counsellors and coaches."

My research revealed that there are two main drivers behind most single expats' decision to move abroad: career and adventure – not necessarily in that order. A job or position abroad can be the perfect break to advance your career. Opportunities open up. The money is better. Many single expats have nothing but adventure on their minds, the call of a life outside their home culture, the lure of exploring a new one, and a chance to expand themselves and learn and grow. Whatever the call is for singles, they still need to approach the decision with care. Here's how.

### Make a Broad List of Decision Factors

You're a single expat, and you want adventure. Perhaps you want to climb the Himalayas, learn Spanish in a village in Central America or snorkel the reefs in the Philippines. You don't have children to worry about or even a partner. You can do whatever you want. You are actively looking for a professional opportunity that will land you near the adventure you so crave. It's exciting and easy to get carried away. Or maybe you are focused on advancing your career and your employer makes you an attractive offer to join the company's brand-new Beijing office, a once-in-a-lifetime opportunity. You say yes immediately and start looking for a Mandarin tutor. What else is there to think about? In fact, a lot. For single expats, the urge to make sudden decisions without forethought is strong. Let's talk about how to decide on what's right for you, both now and in the long term.

- **Values compatibility.** Before making a decision, establish what is important to you, what your core values and needs are, and whether those are compatible with the destination you are considering. Think also in terms of the different dimensions of home and whether your destination provides what you need to feel at home. Look especially at **Table 6.2** in Chapter 6 to get some ideas about how to do that.
- **Long-term horizon.** Also in Chapter 6, I encouraged you to consider how the move fits with your long-term goals and plans. This is even more crucial for a single expat, simply because there are so many possibilities, and it's easy to get caught up in a quest for adventure, career or other, and not think much beyond that. Considering the different areas of your life – health, career, friends and family, leisure, personal development, romance or others – how does a move fit with your long-term goals in each area?
- **Financials.** Consider whether the move is financially viable for you. What is the relationship between your projected earnings and the cost of living at your potential destination? Are you able to sustain yourself or will you end up operating at a deficit? If the financial aspect is important to you, will the move improve your situation?
- **Single-friendliness.** Some destinations are more popular with single people than others. Are there opportunities

for single people to socialize and/or date (if relevant) at your new location? Are there activities targeted specifically at singles? Single-friendliness also includes societal and cultural attitudes towards single people. Are you likely to feel accepted and comfortable? To give an example, the Gulf region is believed to be extremely family-friendly (given the value that the Arab culture places on family), but it is not particularly welcoming to singles, especially single women. By contrast, Thailand tends to be a popular destination for single expats of both sexes.

- **Safety and security.** Find out about local customs, social norms, and attitudes and how they will affect you. Are you moving to a culture and society that is likely to be unfriendly or even dangerous for you? Are you likely to be viewed negatively, discriminated against, be subject to violence or even get in trouble with the law, based on your gender identity, race, sexual preference or other minority status? For instance, according to Human Rights Watch, some 80 countries have anti-LGBT laws, 60% of which can impose prison sentences of up to 10 years, and 7.6% even the death penalty.[4] Before Oliver, the British expat we met in Chapter 4, accepted the assignment in Hong Kong, he had turned down one in a Middle Eastern country, because, he said, "I did not want to move somewhere where I either felt unsafe or had to lead a secret life in order to stay safe." If you are a single woman, be sure to know how you are likely to be treated in your new host culture, including your legal rights and obligations. If you are still considering a move despite an unfriendly cultural climate, at least be aware of the trade-offs.

- **Your own resilience.** Moving as a single person can be taxing emotionally. Are you prepared to deal with this? What are your sources of strength and comfort, which will allow you to handle the first few months of intensified loneliness (exacerbated by the non-familiarity of your surroundings), during the time it takes to adjust to the new way of life? Refer back to Chapter 3 for strategies that help you develop resilience.

- **Your need for support.** You will need a support network to help you cope with the transition. How much support do you need and are you prepared to be proactive about setting that up by yourself? How far out of your comfort zone are you prepared to go to do that? Knowing yourself, your limits and needs will help you determine the kind of support you will need.

There may be other factors that will influence your decision, so take the time to identify them. Talk to other single people at your destination when deciding. But don't let fear stop you. Many singles lead successful expat lives all across the globe. Get online and find forums and Meetups where you can connect with such people. Get to know the 'how' and 'what' of the adventure you want to have. This is a great way to meet 'partners in adventure', people with whom you can travel the country with, ski with and visit ruins. They'll be able to help you with your questions, from day-to-day life to logistics and personal safety.

## Negotiate the Right Kind of Support
Let your employer help you. For instance:

- Don't hesitate to request the services of a relocation consultant. The amount of paperwork required for relocation can be daunting, especially when you have to handle it all yourself, while working full time. Ask for help in dealing with bureaucratic matters (visas, permits, travel documents) early on, so that you are all set up by the time you are ready to move.
- Ask for cross-cultural training geared to your specific circumstances and needs as a single person in the new location.

This should include coaching on social norms, cultural attitudes towards singles and dating guidelines, as well as recommendations on activities, where to meet other single people and others.

See Chapter 7 for potential additional support you can request from your employer, for instance, language training or psychological support from a qualified mental health professional if you need it.

## WHEN PREPARING

Susan had months to prepare for her move to Tokyo, but no one to ask any questions. What followed after the move was an extended period of confusion as she settled into her job, found a place to live and met other expats. The planning phase is relatively straightforward for singles. You only need to consider one set of implications and plan for yourself only. However, while there are fewer decisions to be made and tasks to be carried out, there is also only one person to make them. And sometimes the excitement and lack of anything holding you back may make you want to leap before you look. How can you best prepare for your single move?

### Establish Your Priorities

What details do you most need to settle upfront and what can wait for a later point in time? Your first priority should be taking care of the legalities and paperwork (permits, bank accounts, health insurance). Then figure out your other priorities – whether these are setting up your home, scheduling your first adventure, getting up to speed at work, creating a social circle or other. Make a list and then work it.

## Table 10.1: Priorities for the Move

| |
|---|
| 1. |
| 2. |
| 3. |
| 4. |
| 5. |

## When Looking for Housing, Set Yourself Up for Success

When David made his first solo move to Toronto, right after graduating from university, he felt daunted at the prospect of living in a big city. "When friends of my parents offered to rent me a basement flat, it somehow felt more familiar and safe and I went for it." However, the flat was far from the city centre and David ended up feeling isolated and depressed in his first months there. "I did not know any people in Toronto, so I would come home from work and spend my evenings alone. There weren't any cafés or restaurants around, nowhere to meet people. I had no social life and no chance of developing one." David left after a year and moved to a flat in the centre of town, where he was much happier.

Look for something close to where other singles live, in a nice neighbourhood, near restaurants, bars, shops or other opportunities to meet people, even if you have to compromise on the kind of dwelling or have a longer commute to work. Your social life will thank you.

Also, when considering housing, keep safety in mind – certain neighbourhoods may not be safe for a single person.

How far is the train station from where you live? What roads will you have to walk down at night when you get off work? Many single women choose to live in a building with tight security, perhaps even a security guard in 'riskier' countries. Some people choose to live in gated communities for the extra safety. Make sure, once inside your potential new home, that doors lock securely. Figure out the laundry service. Would you want to have to go to the basement alone to do your laundry at night after a long day of work? Probably not.

Think, too, about the size of the place you choose to live in. How often will you be home? How much room are you going to need? Expats coming from cultures where homes are large often rent places that are far bigger than they need, ending up in a large lonely space. A smaller place is also much easier to take care of.

Singles often go out to eat after a busy day. What restaurants are near your home? What kinds of food do you prefer? Singles also tend to hire more help, use laundry and dry-cleaning services more often, order take-out daily, hire cleaners to do everything – make sure you live in an area where you can get the support you need.

## Line Up Practical Support for the Moving Phase

Moves are physically taxing, all the more so when you have to do it all alone. Make sure you have enough support, and don't end up moving boxes or furniture yourself. Talk to your corporate sponsor about the moving company that will be packing you up and moving you to your new destination. Arrange for as much help as they will provide, especially if you expect to be very busy at work the first few weeks.

## Budget Time to Settle in Before Starting Work

If the move is demanding, and you can't get help from friends, family or even acquaintances to help you unpack and settle into your new place, set aside more time between the physical move and the day you have to start your new position.

## Prioritize Building Up Your Support Network

I have already emphasized the importance of starting to build your support network before you make the actual move. This is even more important if you are a single expat because you will have to do it alone and it will therefore take more time. Also, it helps immensely to have something in place already before you move, so that you don't end up completely isolated during your first weeks and months in your new home.

There are a few things that are particularly helpful when you are moving solo. First, have a contact person upon arrival, so you don't feel lost and alone. Try to connect with one or more of your colleagues already on location, ideally including some who also are single. They can guide you to where the real adventure is, while also helping you navigate day-to-day mundane tasks. See if someone would agree to meet you as soon as you arrive. You can also ask your employer to set you up with a local mentor or host. Connect with expat groups based at your destination well before your move. Chapter 7 on preparation has several ideas on how to start the work of getting connected in the planning phase.

## WHEN MOVING

Singles, more than any other group, have the luxury of moving with fewer possessions and complications concerning timing and coordination. Depending on your personality, you can move with few to no possessions or only bring those objects that you know you will need to feel at home at your new destination. Look at your belongings and decide what really needs to go with you. What is essential for you to create home in your new location?

Andreas commutes every week from his base in Vienna, where his wife and children live, to Berlin, where he rents a small apartment for himself. "I had an offer for a permanent hotel room, which would have cost the same as the apartment and probably would have been much more convenient. Even though the apartment is only equipped with the basics (I'm not the kind of person who would invest in furniture since I don't spend a lot of time there anyway), I have some pictures on the wall and it somehow feels like home."

Susan, the single who got off to a rough start in Japan, says she has gotten down to two roller suitcases of possessions twice in her life, putting the rest in storage in her home country. "I look for furnished flats. I carry a few special knick-knacks and pictures with me. I prefer to purchase extra clothes when I get there because whatever they have in the shops there will be more appropriate to the environment than anything I could bring from home." And when the assignment ends, you have to think about getting the possessions back to your home country. For many, this lesson on the advantages of moving sparingly doesn't sink in until the second or third move.

Whatever your specific needs, the basic challenges of moving as a single expat are fewer than those of a family move. However, Ann, a single Swedish expat interviewee, told me, "There is less to handle, but you must handle everything." You have less stuff, but more work packing and unpacking by yourself. And, when it comes to moving your stuff alone, large, heavy-duty boxes should be left for professionals. "I wish I hadn't packed 20 litres of (vegan) milk in a box that I had to carry up to my third-floor apartment."

You have to figure out logistics for you and not for several other people, but you have to take care of them yourself. That said, some of the logistics of moving, such as finding accommodation, setting up utilities, giving notices and cancelling subscriptions, are the same whether you move alone or with a family.

## Start Packing Early and Enlist the Help of Your Friends

Depending on how much support you have, budget enough time to clean out your possessions, decide what goes and what stays, and make sure you have your essentials handy. Ask your friends for help, at least with packing on the one side. See Chapter 8 for more detailed suggestions on how to manage the moving process.

## Make Self-Care a Priority

Moving is physically and emotionally demanding. As a single person, you have to monitor yourself, especially when you're tempted to work longer hours in the first few months of your new job. Consider questions such as: How will I cope with stress? How will I make sure to eat healthy and sleep enough? Where and when will I be able to exercise? Schedule time off and be disciplined about taking breaks. Arrange for activities that help you decompress, whether that's jogging or going to a movie or listening to a meditation app on your phone. Use whatever methods have worked for you in the past. Can you subscribe to a video series of yoga classes that you bring with you and do regularly for continuity? Any exercise or practice you did at home, when brought to your new destination, will provide you with a comforting sense of continuity.

## Connect with Your Support Network Back Home

Your existing network is your lifeline in the initial time after your move. Plan now to line up that support, when needed. Schedule regular calls with your family and friends back home for those first few weeks. If you have a coach or a therapist, check if they are willing and prepared do phone or video sessions after you move, if you need them or until you find someone local. Remember, you will be having great adventures and will want to talk about yourself when you connect with your old friends or family, but make sure you take the time to listen to *their* stories, and to be there for them. It's easy to alienate old friends as you move on with your life.

## WHEN SETTLING IN

Most single expats I surveyed found settling in to be the toughest phase of moving. Similar to the other phases, being on your own has advantages. You are not responsible for anyone else's adjustment, and therefore are under less pressure to make the move successful than someone moving with a partner or family. At the same time, you may have more time and space to focus on yourself and tend to your own needs and wellbeing. Still, because you are only focusing on yourself, it's easy to become too introspective. You will have more time to focus on work, which is a big advantage, especially in your first few weeks and months, but you want to make sure that you also build a social life.

Foremost among the unique challenges single expats face during the settling-in phase is not having the support that a partner or a family would provide. In practical terms, for example, setting up your physical home is harder when you are on your own. Apart from the fact that you will likely be working long hours and have less time to devote to it, as one of my single interview partners put it: "You struggle even to hang up a painting by yourself" without someone there to tell you if it's well centred and straight.

You also need to set up your whole new local support system by yourself, again, most likely having limited time due to your work obligations. You don't have a partner to share the burden. This is why it is so important to do a lot of the preparatory work ahead of your move.

More importantly, it may be difficult to secure all the emotional support that you need. Friends and family back home can be there for you, and your expat mentor, if you have one, will help, but you will have to carry a lot of the emotional weight yourself. Especially in the first few months until you meet a new circle of friends, and especially if you spend long hours at the office, you may feel lonely and isolated. "Shopping and going out alone," "loneliness at mealtimes" and "not having plans for the weekend" are some of the challenges the single expats I've surveyed mentioned, in addition to not having someone at home "to share your daily experiences and discoveries," "process the changes and confusion," or "turn to when things go wrong." That's why building your social circle and new community as early as possible is so crucial.

Feeling safe and comfortable in your new environment is another aspect of the process of settling in. As a single expat, you sometimes have to deal with how society sees you (and single people in general). Veronica, an American expat, remembers how she felt on some of her moves: "The host culture may have certain perceptions of you as a young single woman. I battled with host cultures thinking that I was distanced from my family or had no family since I was alone abroad ... which could not be further from the truth!" It's not always easy to tell in advance how you will be perceived or treated, so you may end up discovering and having to deal with those once you are on location.

Despite all these challenges, with a little advance planning and awareness of the challenges, you can ensure a smooth transition to your new life as a single expat. With the right attention to detail, you can make it a worthwhile experience, and there is no better avenue for personal growth than having your resourcefulness challenged. Here are some key priorities you need to focus on when settling in.

## Make Your New Residence a Home

We already discussed strategies for doing that in previous chapters, especially Chapter 9. Set up not only your physical home as soon as possible, but also try to establish routines immediately. Find out where to go for a drink, where to buy groceries, where to shop after-hours. Start building a sense of normalcy.

## Prioritize Your Social Life

As soon as you can, get out to places that are not work or your new residence. Walk. Meet people and connect. Have people over. Don't rely on the one person you know. Have a conscious strategy and plan for meeting people. Use online platforms, such as expat forums or Meetup groups. Join expat groups in your location that are targeted at singles and encourage face-to-face interaction, such as Internations, Girls Gone International and others. See Chapter 7 on the preparation phase for ideas on how to jumpstart your social life.

Lori, an American expat, thinks back to her first few weeks in Johannesburg. "I wish I had made a plan for meeting people, meaning that I wish I'd challenged myself to meet a new person for coffee once a week. I expected that to happen organically. At a certain age, it doesn't anymore. People are settled around you and you have to make an effort to connect." Say yes to every invitation, even if it's not the greatest event of the year. Getting out is a muscle you need to build.

Also, although having *any* friends is huge, make sure you connect with at least a few single friends. Sometimes you will need someone who does not have obligations to a partner or family or can spontaneously go out with you and, most important, understands exactly how you feel.

## Stay Safe

Lori shared with me another story. "I was in a cab in Sao Paolo. I was feeling particularly lonely. The cab driver asked me if I was visiting. I replied 'no' and started telling him about my job, about working late all the time, and pretty much told him what I would tell a friend. He responded by saying, 'I am a nice man and I am going to give you advice as if you were my daughter. Find a friend and tell them about all that. If I were a bad person, I could get you robbed.' He was indeed a kind man, but he reminded me that, although I was longing for conversation, I needed to be mindful of my own safety when doing so."

When you live alone, even within your home country, you may have to take care not to end up in dangerous situations, especially (but not exclusively) if you are a single woman. In a foreign, unfamiliar environment, this may get magnified. Being single is a great opportunity to meet many different and interesting people. Be aware and take precautions, but don't let fear stop you from living your dream.

## Take the Time to Feel Normal

When Julie moved from her hometown in Indiana to Vienna, Austria, she remembers how hectic her first few days were. "About a week or so after moving, I was running around trying to get phone service, internet, work permits and utilities set up. I didn't speak German, kept getting lost and the bureaucracy was driving me crazy. At one point, as I walked down the sidewalk, I accidentally stepped into dog poo. That was the last straw! I was tired, frustrated, lonely and feeling terribly incompetent. As the tears ran down my cheeks, a question popped into my head, 'What do I need so that I can feel normal?' I decided it was to relax with a cup of coffee and something in English to read. So, I stopped at the corner news stand and bought the *Wall Street Journal*, the only English thing they had, and went to a cute little café nearby. After about 30 minutes I was able to pull myself together, gather up my courage again and get back to my errands. I learned a valuable lesson that day. Don't forget to take the time to feel normal. It will get you through the challenging times."

What traditions can you recreate that will allow you to feel normal? For Susan, when she moved to London, it was finding Mexican food and listening to rap music, because they both reminded her of home. "I had no idea I'd miss these things when I moved!" she remembers.

Travelling as a single person can teach you courage, show you how capable you are, strip away expectations and social conditioning and reveal your core values, propel your career in different directions, turn you into a global citizen and help you find a whole new tribe. To quote author David Mitchell, "Travel far enough, you meet yourself."[5] Take the time you have as a single person to go within and find yourself, and take the risks you may not be able to take when you have a partner or a family.

# CHECKLIST

- Have you taken the time to identify all the factors that you should take into account in deciding to make a move? Are there people – other expats, relocation specialists, family and friends – who can help you think through your decision?

- Have you identified the full range of potential support your employer can provide, including not just the standard support for moving and finding housing, but also help in dealing with all the bureaucratic issues and cultural adjustment?

- Have you thought through the choices and trade-offs associated with deciding where to live, including not just the time to get to work, but also proximity to activities you like and other singles?

- Have you enlisted the support of friends and family to help you pack (and, if possible, unpack)?

- Have you factored in time for self-care and for getting oriented in your new location?

# CON
# CLU
# SION

YOUR GREAT MOVE

*"Ma patrie est une valise,
ma valise, ma patrie.
(My homeland is a suitcase,
my suitcase, my homeland.)"*

**Mahmoud Darwich** (excerpt)

You now know what it takes to make a great expat move – from decision to planning and preparation, to moving and finally, settling into your new home. You've read about how others, expats like you, have coped with some of the most common challenges. You've learned from their mistakes and are aware of potential pitfalls and how to avoid them. You're clear on key priorities, principles, strategies and steps. You're ready to take action.

Before you do, though, take a step back and reconnect with your intention. What's your 'why' for making this particular move, and also for taking on the journey of expatriation? This is important because it should be the unifying theme for all the transitions you (and your family) will experience. It will anchor you as you proceed through each phase of a move and experience the inevitable highs and the lows. It will provide you with a sense of consistency and continuity across phases – and across moves. Your intention also connects you to your longer-term plan – where you are, where you want to be next and how you will get there. While unexpected events are inevitable and you will need to be flexible, it's important that you have a plan in the first place.

Moving and starting a new life abroad is an exciting, terrifying, rewarding, frustrating, enriching and challenging, but above all, life-changing experience. Whatever phase you are currently in – whether you are settling into a new home, waiting for the movers to come pack your belongings, exploring housing and schooling options in a new country, deciding whether to accept an expat assignment or even just considering whether the expat lifestyle is for you – here are some key ideas from this book that will help you make *your* great move.

## WHAT YOU NEED TO KNOW TO MAKE A GREAT MOVE

1. **Don't decide lightly.** Decide in haste, suffer at leisure. Moving and living abroad will change more than your address, the currency you use or your health insurance provider. It will change your life. Give your decision the consideration and importance it deserves. Get your partner on board.

2. **Know what to expect.** Having realistic expectations is key to moving successfully through the process of transition. Starting at the decision-making phase, it's crucial to know the basic parameters of your new existence – the implications for every area of your life. Do your research and be prepared. Check your assumptions.

3. **Understand what you need to create home.** Moving and adjusting to a new environment is about creating your new home. Your efforts are much more intentional, coherent and systematic when you are clear about what everyone who moves needs to feel at home.

4. **Don't do it alone.** Having appropriate support makes a huge difference in each phase of the moving process. Know what kind of support you need and ask for it or set it up. Leverage your existing support network. Start early and invest in building your new one.

5. **Know yourself and those with whom you move.** Personality and experience will powerfully shape how you adjust to your new life. Awareness of those elements will help

you anticipate and get the support you and your loved ones need to make a successful transition.

6. **Anticipate the adjustment process.** Keep the stages of transition always in your mind as you move through the process. They will help you keep perspective about what's ahead and also help you manage your expectations.

7. **Find your tribe.** Community matters. It can shape how you experience and adjust to your new life. Nurture ties to your existing network, but don't forget that the sooner you create a new community and have a sense of belonging, the faster you will feel at home in your new location.

8. **Prioritize your family.** They need as much, or even more, support than you do. Their happiness and wellbeing through the moving and settling-in phases are directly linked to your own – and to the overall success of your expat assignment.

9. **Engage in self-care.** Things will get intense, sometimes even overwhelming. The best way to cope is by being kind to yourself, staying healthy and even indulging yourself from time to time.

## PREPARE TO BE CHANGED

Living abroad teaches you a lot about yourself. Abigail, an American, followed her husband on a two-year expat assignment in Vienna, Austria, with only basic knowledge of German. In the beginning, she felt very much like a foreigner. "Things like going to the grocery store, a restaurant, the doctor … I was very shy to use the language, so I struggled with communication. As I grew more comfortable, I was able to make myself understood and get things done. When that happened, I was so proud of myself! I was much more self-confident and in control of my own destiny. If you had asked me ten years ago if I would see myself living and functioning in a language other than my native English, I would have said 'No way!'"

More important, living abroad irreversibly changes you. The very act of moving away from your home environment and culture will bring out qualities in you that you did not know you possessed. You may become more patient, more sensitive to cultural nuances, more tolerant of differences. Like Abigail, you will discover that you are capable of much more than you thought.

Over time, the expat experience may even shift some of your basic character traits. For example, going through change and adjustment may make you more open to new experiences. Sometimes, you may even be more open to taking risks you did not have the courage to take before, because you know that you can handle them. When you have stepped out of your comfort zone once (or twice) already, you become less hesitant to do it again.

How you behave in a social setting may also change. In familiar surroundings, where you have a social circle and support system, you may not have such a strong impulse to reach out to others. In a new environment, you may have no choice but to reach out to people rather than wait for them to come to you. Even if that is out of character, it may be essential for you to cope with the challenges of setting up a new life in an unfamiliar location. In the process, you learn to build relationships with people of different backgrounds, characters and mentality. You also, again, build confidence in yourself and your ability to overcome your own barriers. This may become part of the 'new you'.

Moving away from your familiar surroundings and the comfort of doing things a certain way can also open up new options, professional and personal. Unconstrained by your usual frame of reference, you may become more creative and willing to consider less traditional avenues to attain your goals. Maybe your goals themselves will change. Perhaps you will change career directions or decide to develop a portable career. Perhaps what started as a one-time adventure will turn into a lifestyle choice. We saw examples of all that in this book.

If you decide to live abroad, you need to mentally be ready to change, at a core level. Your identity will shift. The country, the culture, the language, the people, the life you leave behind – they are all part of that identity. Moving away from the context in which that identity was formed and adapting to a new context, you may discover parts of yourself that are new. Others may see you differently too.

Your sense of belonging will shift. So, too, will your home. You may find pieces of home in many different places, without feeling entirely at home in any of them. You may feel nostalgic for the place you used to call home, but when you're there, you may feel out of sync. Your new home may have more to do with love, connection, happy moments and the people with whom you can be your authentic self, rather than geography. This home you will carry with you wherever you go.

You need to be prepared for all those changes because, as a good friend of mine likes to say, "Once an expat, always an expat."

I hope this book will help you make your expat journey as exciting, rewarding, meaningful and smooth as possible. Make the most of it. Go out and thrive. Make many great moves and find your home in the world.

# APPENDIX

The following table is an example of how to organize and keep track of key tasks for an international move. It is organized by time and location. Feel free to use it as a template and tailor to your own needs and circumstances. For 'status', you can colour code – for instance, green for 'done' and yellow for 'in-process'.

## Moving Checklist – ORIGIN

| What | Who | By When | Status |
|---|---|---|---|
| **As soon as you have your moving date (ideally three months before moving date)** | | | |
| Agree on moving date(s) | | | |
| Contact moving companies for quotes and set up appointments | | | |
| Choose moving company. Set date for physical move | | | |
| Fill out required paperwork | | | |
| Verify immigration and documentation requirements | | | |
| Fill out immigration paperwork/apply for visa(s), residence and work permit(s) | | | |
| Check passport validity; renew, if necessary | | | |
| Find out vaccination requirements, if any | | | |
| *If you have pets:* Verify quarantine and documentation requirements and make arrangements to move them | | | |
| Book travel to destination | | | |
| Arrange for temporary accommodation at origin (after belongings are packed) | | | |
| Arrange for temporary accommodation at destination (until belongings arrive) | | | |
| *If renting:* Give notice/terminate rental agreement effective [date] | | | |
| *If you own your home and are selling or renting out:* Put property on the market (as an individual or through an agency) | | | |
| Identify what (furniture, appliances, personal items) goes with you and what will be sold/donated/given away/stored | | | |

| | | | |
|---|---|---|---|
| Advertise furniture for sale/make arrangements for disposing of or storing other items | | | |
| Decide on and buy new furniture, if necessary | | | |
| Decide on vehicle(s) to take/sell | | | |
| Terminate vehicle insurances and registration effective [date] | | | |
| End electricity, gas, mobile phone/fixed line/internet contracts effective [date] | | | |
| Agree on separation with household employee(s) | | | |
| Terminate social security | | | |
| Review personal health insurance/transfer to destination | | | |
| Check and verify pension transfer arrangements | | | |
| Notify tax authorities and finalize taxes | | | |
| Cancel household insurance, effective [moving date] Cancel other insurances effective [date] | | | |
| Inform school(s) of your move – arrange for potential record transfer to new school | | | |
| Research social networks and groups at your destination | | | |
| Research favorite activities at your destination | | | |
| Set up meeting with international lawyer and/or tax specialist. Get information on legal status and rights at destination | | | |
| **Two months before moving date or as soon as you have your new address** | | | |
| Arrange mail forwarding at post office | | | |
| Change address for subscriptions, banks and wherever else needed | | | |

| Task | | | | | |
|---|---|---|---|---|---|
| Cancel magazine/newspaper subscriptions and deliveries or change address | | | | | |
| Cancel non-transferable memberships | | | | | |
| Sort and clean out your possessions | | | | | |
| Decide what goes by air and what by land/sea (if relevant) | | | | | |
| Organize doctors' appointments or medical checkups (e.g. dental cleaning) | | | | | |
| Get originals of medical records or arrange transfer | | | | | |
| **One month before moving date** | | | | | |
| *If renting:* Arrange apartment or house hand-over | | | | | |
| Make copies of important documents and keep originals in safe location | | | | | |
| Dissolve bank accounts and transfer funds, if relevant | | | | | |
| Cancel credit cards effective [date] | | | | | |
| Pay outstanding bills before closing bank accounts | | | | | |
| *If retaining accounts or continuing to make payments from your account(s), such as mortgage, loan or other payments:* Set up the system for doing so. Make sure you have online banking access at destination. | | | | | |
| Plan goodbye party | | | | | |
| Make appointments to see friends and family | | | | | |
| Schedule visits to favorite places | | | | | |
| Refill prescription medication. Find out if medication is available at destination and under what name. | | | | | |

| | | | |
|---|---|---|---|
| Get supplies of products that you are not likely to find (or are more expensive) at destination | | | |
| One week before moving date | | | |
| Confirm with moving company | | | |
| Pack an 'essentials' box/have your kids pack their 'essentials' backpacks | | | |
| Have goodbye party | | | |
| Provide your friends and family with your forwarding address and new contact details | | | |
| Arrange for child care and organize meals for moving day | | | |
| Arrange for cleaning service for your place after movers leave | | | |

## Moving Checklist – DESTINATION

| What | Who | By When | Status |
|---|---|---|---|
| **As soon as you have your moving date (ideally three months before moving date)** | | | |
| Schedule, book and organize look-see visit | | | |
| Decide on accommodation | | | |
| Sign rental contract | | | |
| Get phone/Internet for your new home | | | |
| Set up utilities for your new home | | | |
| Get mobile phone contract(s) | | | |
| Buy or lease vehicle | | | |
| Purchase vehicle insurance | | | |

Find out if your existing driver's license is valid in the new location. If not, find out the procedure for obtaining an international or local license

Open bank accounts)

Select school/day care

Register children for school

**Two months before moving date or as soon as you have your new address**

Organize child care – interview and hire

Interview and hire household help or other personnel, if relevant

Register with social security

Purchase health insurance

Clarify tax status at destination

Set up household, accident and other insurances in the new location

Find a primary care physician, pediatrician, other specialists

**One month before moving date**

Get in touch with acquaintances in the new location and set up meetings for when you're there

Find out about events at your destination and schedule some for when you're there

Join an expat (or other) club

Join a gym (or sign up for other activities)

Register children for activities

Schedule regular calls with family and friends

# ENDNOTES

## INTRODUCTION

1. "Global Expatriates: Size, Segmentation and Forecast for the Worldwide Market." Finaccord (2014). Accessed February 13, 2018. http://finaccord.com/uk/report_global-expatriates_size-segmentation-and-forecast-for-the-worldwide-market.html.

2. "Talent Mobility 2020: The Next Generation of International Assignments." PricewaterhouseCoopers LLP (2010): 4. Accessed February 13, 2018. http://www.pwc.com/gx/en/managing-tomorrows-people/future-of-work/pdf/talent-mobility-2020.pdf.

3. "2016 Global Mobility Trends." Brookfield GRS (2016): 48. Accessed February 13, 2018. http://globalmobilitytrends.bgrs.com

4. "Millennials at Work: Reshaping the Workplace." PricewaterhouseCoopers LLP (2011): 5. Accessed 28 November, 2017. https://www.pwc.com/m1/en/services/consulting/documents/millennials-at-work.pdf.

5. "Measuring the Value of International Assignments." PricewaterhouseCoopers LLP and Cranfield University School of Management (2006): 18-20. Accessed 28 November, 2017. https://www.pwc.fi/fi/palvelut/tiedostot/pwc_measuring_the_value.pdf.

6. Rob Gray. "How to Get the Most Out of Global Mobility." *HR Magazine* (2014). Accessed February 13, 2018. http://www.hrmagazine.co.uk/article-details/how-to-get-the-most-out-of-global-mobility.

7. "International Mobility and Dual Career Survey of International Employers." Permits Foundation (2012): 8. Accessed February 13, 2018. https://www.permitsfoundation.com/wp-content/uploads/2013/04/Permits-Global-Employers-Survey-2012.pdf. Also see PricewaterhouseCoopers and Cranfield University School of Management (2006): 16.

8. Brookfield GRS (2016): 50.

## INTENTION AND THE RIGHT PRINCIPLES

1. Vineet Nayar. "The Power of Intention." *Harvard Business Review* (2013). Accessed February 13, 2018. https://hbr.org/2013/02/the-power-of-intent

## CHAPTER 1

1. Anand Giridharadas. "The Struggle of the Global Placeless." *New York Times* (2010). Accessed February 13, 2018. http://www.nytimes.com/2010/03/27/us/27iht-currents.html.

2. Salman Rushdie. *Imaginary Homelands: Essays and Criticism 1981-1991* (New York: Penguin Books, 1992).

3. Morgan W. McCall, Morgan W and George P. Hollenbeck. *Developing Global Executives: The Lessons of International Experience* (Boston: Harvard Business School Press, 2002).

4. Norma McCaig also coined the term 'global nomad' in Norma McCaig. "Growing Up with a World View." *US Foreign Service Journal* (1994): 32-41.

5. Ibid.

6. Pico Iyer. *The Global Soul: Jet Lag, Shopping Malls and the Search for Home* (New York: Alfred A. Knopf, 2000).

7. Pico Iyer. "Living in the Transit Lounge." Chapter in Faith Eidse and Nina Sichel (eds.). Unrooted Childhoods: Memoirs of Growing Up Global (London: Nicholas Brealey Publishing, 2004).

8. Susan J. Matt. *Homesickness: An American History* (New York: Oxford University Press, 2011): 267.

9. Ibid: 254.

10. Susan J. Matt. "The New Globalist is Homesick," *New York Times* (2012). Accessed February 13, 2018. http://www.nytimes.com/2012/03/22/opinion/many-still-live-with-homesickness.html.

## CHAPTER 2

1. "Expat Explorer: Achieving Ambitions Abroad."
   HSBC Global Report (2016). Accessed February 13, 2018.
   https://www.expatexplorer.hsbc.com/survey/files/pdfs/overall-reports/2016/HSBC_Expat_Explorer_2016_report.pdf

2. Sverre Lysgaard. "Adjustment in a Foreign Society: Norwegian Fulbright Grantees Visiting the United States,"
   *International Social Science Bulletin* (1955), 7: 45-51.

3. David Kessler. "The five stages of grief." Grief.com. Accessed February 13, 2018. https://grief.com/the-five-stages-of-grief/.

## CHAPTER 3

1. The Newcastle Personality Assessor is a 10-question personality test created by Daniel Nettle, a behavioural scientist at the Centre for Behaviour & Evolution, Newcastle University, and author of the book *Personality: What Makes You the Way You Are* (Oxford, UK: Oxford University Press, 2007).

2. "Power of Personality." Accessed February 13, 2018. http://www.facet5global.com/.

3. Paul T. Costa, Jr. and Robert R. McCrae. "DNEO PI-3" Sigma Assessment Systems (2010). Accessed February 13, 2018. http://www.sigmaassessmentsystems.com/assessments/neo-personality-inventory-3/.

4. Meredith Downes, Iris I. Varner and Hemmasi Masoud. "Individual Profiles as Predictors of Expatriate Effectiveness," *Competitiveness Review*, Vol. 20, No.3 (2010): 235-247. Although the study was geared towards the corporate world (the selection of employees for expatriate assignments), its applicability is much broader. The Downes, et al., study used the Big Five personality traits as a basis for determining the influence of personality on expatriate adjustment. For an overview of the Big Five, see Nettle (2007).

5. Paula M. Caligiuri. "Selecting Expatriates for Personality Charac-
   teristics: A Moderating Effect of Personality on the Relationship
   Between Host National Contact and Cross-Cultural Adjustment,"
   *Management International Review*, Vol. 40, No. 1 (2000): 61-80.
   Accessed April 23, 2018. https://pdfs.semanticscholar.org/4963/
   cc4396dfa50e4dcc3500019e53ee9870501f.pdf.

   For a more extensive look at the early literature on personality
   and expatriate assimilation/assignment success, see Karen
   V. Beaman. "Myths, Mystiques and Mistakes in Overseas
   Assignments: The Role of Global Mindset in International
   Work," *IHRIM Journal* (November/December 2004). Accessed
   February 13, 2018. http://citeseerx.ist.psu.edu/viewdoc/
   download?doi=10.1.1.462.1446&rep=rep1&type=pdf

6. For more information on the concept of Norwegian Folk
   High Schools, see "Welcome." Folke Hogskole. Accessed
   February 13, 2018. https://www.folkehogskole.no/index.
   php?page_id=44.

7. Adapted from "Self-determination Theory (Deci and Ryan)"
   Learning Theories. Accessed February 13, 2018. https://www.learn-
   ing-theories.com/self-determination-theory-deci-and-ryan.html.

8. Maria Konnikova. "How People Learn to Become Resilient," *New Yorker* (2016). Accessed February 13, 2018.
   http://www.newyorker.com/science/maria-konnikova/
   the-secret-formula-for-resilience.

9. Diane L. Coutu. "How Resilience Works," *Harvard
   Business Review* (2002). Accessed February 13, 2018.
   https://hbr.org/2002/05/how-resilience-works.

10. "Up or Out: Next Moves for the Modern Expatriate."
    Economist Intelligence Unit (2010). Accessed February 13, 2018.
    http://graphics.eiu.com/upload/eb/LON_PL_Regus_WEB2.pdf.

11. David Livermore. *The Cultural Intelligence Difference: Master the
    One Skill You Can't Do Without in Today's Global Economy*
    (New York: AMACOM, 2011).

12. Janet M. Bennett and Milton J. Bennett. "Developing Intercultural Sensitivity: An Integrative Approach to Global and Domestic Diversity," paper presented at The Diversity Symposium (2001). Accessed February 13, 2018. http://www.diversitycollegium.org/pdf2001/2001Bennettspaper.pdf.

13. Soon Ang, Linn Van Dyne, Christine Koh, K. Yee Ng, Klaus J. Templer, Cheryl Tay and N. Anand Chandrasekar. "Cultural Intelligence: Its Measurement and Effects on Cultural Judgment and Decision Making, Cultural Adaptation, and Task Performance," *Management and Organization Review* Vol. 3 No. 3 (2007): 335-371. Accessed February 13, 2018. http://www.linnvandyne.com/papers/MOR Ang_Van Dyne etc. 2007.pdf

14. Geert Hofstede. *Cultures and Organisations: Software of the Mind.* (London: McGraw Hill, 1991).

15. "Culture." People.temu.edu. Accessed February 13, 2018. http://www.tamu.edu/faculty/choudhury/culture.html

16. For more details on Hofstede's model, see "National Culture." Hofstede Insights. Accessed February 13, 2018. https://www.hofstede-insights.com/models/national-culture/

17. David Livermore (2011).

18. David Livermore. "Sit Still and Improve Your CQ: The Power of Reflection." Cultural Intelligence Center. Accessed February 13, 2018. https://culturalq.com/sit-still-and-improve-your-cq-the-power-of-reflection/

## CHAPTER 4

1. Robert J. Brown. "Dominant Stressors on Expatriate Couples During International Assignments," The International Journal of Human Resource Management, Vol. 19, No. 6 (2008): 1019. Accessed February 13, 2018. http://www.tandfonline.com/doi/abs/10.1080/09585190802051303

2. "2012 Trends in Global Relocation – Global Mobility Policy and Practices Survey." Cartus (2012).

3. BGRS (2016): 41, 70.

4. Copeland, Anne P. (2004) "Many Women Many Voices," Study of Accompanying Spouses Around the World, conducted by The Interchange Institute and commissioned by Prudential Financial. Accessed February 13, 2018. http://www.interchange-institute.org/files/MWMVFinal05.pdf

5. Brookfield GRS (2016): 50.

6. The terms 'trailing spouse' or 'trailing partner' (referring to the person who follows their partner to another city or country because of a work assignment) seems to have been used first by Mary Bralove in the *Wall Street Journal* on 15 July 1981 in an article titled "Problems of Two-Career Families Start Forcing Businesses to Adapt." Because of the terms' negative connotations, other terms, such as expat partner or accompanying partner, often are preferred. In this book, I use the different terms interchangeably.

7. "Expatriate Spouses and Partners Employment, Work Permits and International Mobility – International Survey Summary Report." Permits Foundation (2013): 2-3. Accessed February 13, 2018. https://www.permitsfoundation.com/wp-content/uploads/2013/04/Spousal-survey-new-style.pdf. Also cited in Economist Intelligence Unit (2010): 14.

8. Brookfield GRS (2016): 69.

9. Permits Foundation (2008): 8.

10. According to BGRS (2016): 69, spouse/partner career concerns were the top reason why assignees decide not to take their partner along on a long-term international assignment.

11. Brown (2008).

12. "Talent Mobility 2020 and Beyond." PricewaterhouseCoopers LLP. Accessed February 13, 2018. https://press.pwc.com/Multimedia/image/Talent-mobility-2020-and-beyond/a/f81b0788-4b81-4fe2-a6d1-b6d279352b32.

13. TheMIGroup "The Trailing Male Spouse." *Relocate Magazine* (2016). Accessed February 13, 2018. https://www.relocatemaga-zine.com/mobility-industry-the-trailing-male-spouse.html.

   Clegg, Alicia. "Tales from Trailing Husbands." *Financial Times* (2013). Accessed February 13, 2018. https://www.ft.com/content/0227c0e0-cdf1-11e2-a13e-00144feab7de.

14. Patrick Monahan. "Supportive Relationships Linked to Will-ingness to Pursue Opportunities." Carnegie Mellon University, Dietrich College of Humanities and Social Sciences (2017). Accessed February 13, 2018. https://www.cmu.edu/dietrich/news/news-stories/2017/august/supportive-spouses-brooke-feeny.html

**CHAPTER 5**

1. "Expat Explorer: Achieving Ambitions Abroad." HSBC Global Report (2016). Accessed February 13, 2018. https://www.expatexplorer.hsbc.com/survey/files/pdfs/overall-reports/2016/HSBC_Expat_Explorer_2016_report.pdf.

2. Sebastian Reiche. "Relocating Children Abroad: The Myths and the Truths." Expatriatus, IESE Business School, University of Navarra (2012). Accessed February 13, 2018. http://blog.iese.edu/expatriatus/2012/12/20/relocating-children-abroad-the-myths-and-the-truths/

3. David Pollock and Ruth Van Reken. *Third Culture Kids: Growing Up Among Worlds, revised edition.* (Boston/London: Nicholas Brealey Publishing, 2009) 75-84.

4. "Expat Child Syndrome (ECS)." Expat Info Desk. Accessed February 13, 2018. https://www.expatinfodesk.com/expat-guide/moving-with-your-children/expat-child-syndrome-ecs/

5. Shigehiro Oishi and Ulrich Shimmack. "Residential Mobility, Well-Being and Mortality." *Journal of Personality and Social Psychology*, Vol. 98, No. 6 (2010): 980-994.

6. Norma McCaig (1994): 32-41.

**CHAPTER 6**

1. Morgan W. McCall and George P. Hollenbeck. *Developing Global Executives: The Lessons of International Experience.* (Boston: Harvard Business School Press, 2002).

2. David Pollock and Ruth Van Reken. (2009): 195-215.

## CHAPTER 7

1. Warwick-Ching. "Ten Worst Mistakes Made by Expats," *Financial Times* (2011). Accessed February 13, 2018. https://www.ft.com/content/f75bc8d8-c3f6-11e0-b302-00144feabdc0

2. "New Research Reveals the Difficulties Faced by Expats," *Relocate Magazine* (2017). Accessed February 13, 2018. https://www.relocatemagazine.com/health-new-research-reveals-the-difficulties-faced-by-expats-.html.

3. Accessed February 13, 2018. http://www.internations.org/

4. Accessed February 13, 2018 https://www.meetup.com/

## CHAPTER 9

1. Kate Berger. "Schools: Helping Expat Kids to Adapt," *Financial Times* (2017). Accessed February 13, 2018. https://propertylistings.ft.com/propertynews/united-kingdom/5132-schools-helping-expat-kids-to-adapt.html

2. Bruce Feiler. "The Stories That Bind Us," *New York Times* (2013). Accessed February 13, 2018. http://www.nytimes.com/2013/03/17/fashion/the-family-stories-that-bind-us-this-life.html

## CHAPTER 10

1. "Profile America Facts for Features: Unmarried and Single Americans Week: September 17-23, 2017." US Census Bureau (2017). Accessed February 13, 2018. https://www.census.gov/newsroom/facts-for-features/2017/single-americans-week.html

2. "The Attraction of Solitude," Economist (2012). Accessed February 13, 2018. http://www.economist.com/node/21560844?frc=ocn/fb/wl/pe/attractionofsolitude

3. Brookfield GRS (2016): 50, 68.

4. Ronald Alsop. "Is This the Most Dangerous Expat Assignment?" BBC Capital (2016). Accessed February 13, 2018. http://www.bbc.com/capital/story/20160331-this-is-the-most-dangerous-expat-assignment

5. David Mitchell. *Cloud Atlas*. (New York: Random House, 2004).

# BIBLIOGRAPHY

## BOOKS

Aciman, André (ed.), *Letters of Transit: Reflections on Exile, Identity, Language and Loss*, New York: The New Press, 1999.

Allen, John S., *Home: How Habitat Made Us Human*, New York: Basic Books, 2015.

Bell, Linda, *Hidden Immigrants: Legacies of Growing Up Abroad*, Notre Dame: Cross Cultural Publications, 1997.

Black, Stewart and Hal B. Gregersen, *So You're Coming Home*, San Diego: Global Business Publishers, 1999.

Blunt, Alison and Robyn Dowling, *Home*, New York: Routlege, 2006.

Brayer Hess, Melissa and Patricia Linderman, *The Expert Expat: Your Guide to Successful Relocation Abroad – Moving, Living, Thriving*, Boston: Nicholas Brealey Publishing, 2007.

Brimm, Linda, *Global Cosmopolitans: The Creative Edge of Difference*, Hampshire: Palgrave Macmillan, 2010.

Bryson, Debra R. and Charise M. Hoge, *A Portable Identity: A Woman's Guide to Maintaining a Sense of Self While Moving Overseas*, Glen Echo: Transition Press International, 2003.

Collins Burgan, Lori, *Moving with Kids: 25 Ways to Ease Your Family's Transition to a New Home*, Boston: The Harvard Common Press, 2007.

De Courtivron, Isabelle, *Lives in Translation: Bilingual Writers on Identity and Creativity*, New York: Palgrave Macmillan, 2003.

Eidse, Faith & Nina Sichel, Eds., *Unrooted Childhoods: Memoirs of Growing Up Global*, London: Nicholas Brealey Publishing, 2004.

Fainlight, Ruth, *New and Collected Poems*, Northumberland: Bloodaxe Books, 2010.

Gallagher, Winifred, *The Power of Place*, New York: Harper Collins, 1993.

Hill, John, *At Home in the World: Sounds and Symmetries of Belonging*, New Orleans: Spring Journal Books, 2010.

Iyer, Pico, *The Global Soul: Jet Lag, Shopping Malls and the Search for Home*, New York: Alfred A. Knopf, 2000.

Iyer, Pico, *The Lady and the Monk: Four Seasons in Kyoto*, New York: Vintage Books, 1992.

Livermore, David, *The Cultural Intelligence Difference: Master the One Skill You Can't Do Without in Today's Global Economy*, New York: AMACOM, 2011.

Malewski, Margaret, *GenExpat: The Young Professional's Guide to Making a Successful Life Abroad*, Yarmouth: Intercultural Press, 2005.

Martins, Andrea and Victoria Hepworth, *Expat Women: Confessions – 50 Answers to Your Real-Life Questions About Living Abroad*, Cotton Tree: Expat Women Enterprises, 2011.

Matt, Susan J., *Homesickness: An American History*, New York: Oxford University Press, 2011.

McCall, Morgan W. and George P. Hollenbeck, *Developing Global Executives: The Lessons of International Experience*, Boston: Harvard Business School Press, 2002. cited in Beaman, 2004.

McTaggart, Lynne, *The Intention Experiment: Using Your Thoughts to Change Your Life and the World*, Free Press, 2007.

Missouri Department of Social Services, *Child Welfare Manual – Chapter 1: Family Systems Theory*, May 13, 2011. http://dss.mo.gov/cd/info/cwmanual/section7/ch1_33/sec7ch1_33.pdf.

Nettle, Daniel, *Personality. What Makes You the Way You Are*, New York: Oxford University Press, 2007.

Pavone, Chris, *The Expats*, New York: Crown Publishing, 2012.

Pollock, David C. and Ruth E. Van Reken, *Third Culture Kids: Growing Up Among Worlds, revised edition*, Boston/London: Nicholas Brealey Publishing, 2009.

Rushdie, Salman, *Imaginary Homelands: Essays and Criticism 1981-1991*, New York: Penguin Books, 1992.

Simens, Julia, *Emotional Resilience and the Expat Child*, Summertime Publishing, 2011.

Storti, Craig, *The Art of Coming Home*, Boston: Intercultural Press (Nicholas Brealy), 2003.

Transler, Catherine, *Turning International: How to Find Happiness and Feel at Home in a New Culture*, Rotterdam: De Zandloper Publications, 2012.

Weiner, Eric, *The Geography of Bliss*, New York: Twelve/Hachette Book Group, 2009.


## REPORTS, ARTICLES, CHAPTERS, BLOG POSTS, PODCASTS, RADIO SHOWS

Angulo, Gracia. "The Many Phases of Being a Lifelong Expat." *Wall Street Journal*, May 11, 2015. https://blogs.wsj.com/expat/2015/05/11/growing-up-on-the-move-the-many-phases-of-being-a-lifelong-expat/.

Ali, Anees Janee. "The Intercultural Adaptation of Expatriate Spouses and Children: an Empirical Study on the Determinants Contributing to the Success of Expatriation." Dissertation, University of Groningen, 2003. https://www.rug.nl/research/portal/publications/the-intercultural-adaptation-of-expatriate-spouses-and-children(51da056a-7bd2-4f8b-be17-60025bf4af24).html.

Ali, Anees et al. "Determinants of Intercultural Adjustment among Expatriate Spouses." *International Journal of Intercultural Relations*, Vol. 27, No. 5 (September 2003): 563-580. http://www.sciencedirect.com/science/article/pii/S0147176703000543.

Alsop, Ronald. "Is This the Most Dangerous Expat Assignment?" *BBC Capital*, March 31, 2016. http://www.bbc.com/capital/story/20160331-this-is-the-most-dangerous-expat-assignment.

Anderson, Monika. "A 'Look-See' Tip List: What to Do on the Visit Before the Big Expat Move." *Wall Street Journal*, March 19, 2015.

Ang, S. et al. "Cultural Intelligence: Its Measurement and Effects on Cultural Judgment and Decision Making, Cultural Adaptation, and Task Performance." *Management and Organization Review*, Vol. 3 No. (2007): 335-371. http://www.linnvandyne.com/papers/ MOR Ang_Van Dyne etc. 2007.pdf.

"A Sense of Place: Genetics and Travel." *Wordgeyser*, February 18, 2013. http://wordgeyser. com/2013/02/18/a-sense-of-place-genetics-and-travel/.

Barker Eric. "How to Make Friends as an Adult: 5 Secrets Backed by Research." *Barking Up The Wrong Tree*, February 2017. http://www.bakadesuyo.com/2017/02/ how-to-make-friends-as-an-adult/.

Beaman, Karen V. "Myths, Mystiques and Mistakes in Overseas Assignments: The Role of Global Mindset in International Work." *IHRIM Journal*, November/December 2004. https://www.researchgate.net/publication/238103015_Myths_ Mystiques_and_Mistakes_The_Role_of_the_Global_Mind-set_in_Building_an_Effective_Multicultural_Workforce.

Beauregard, Mary. "Managing the Shock of Re-entry." *Expatica*, January 17, 2007. http://www.expatica.com/hr/story/ managing-the-shock-of-re-entry-35625.html.

Beck, Julie. "How Friends Become Closer." *The Atlantic*, August 29, 2017. https://www.theatlantic.com/health/ archive/2017/08/how-friends-become-closer/538092/.

"Being Foreign: The Others." *Economist*, December 19, 2009. http://www.economist.com/node/15108690.

Bennett, Janet. "Developing Intercultural Competence." Conference Workshop, 2011 Association of International Education Administrators (AIEA) Conference, San Francisco, CA: February 22, 2011. http://www.pindex.com/uploads/ post_docs/1Analytic-ICIInterculturalCompetence(PIN DEX-DOC-14711).pdf.

Bennett, Janet M. and Milton J. Bennett. "Developing Intercultural Sensitivity: An Integrative Approach to Global and Domestic Diversity." Paper presented at The Diversity Symposium 2001. http://www.diversitycollegium.org/pdf2001/2001Bennettspaper.pdf.

Benzel, Jan. "If You Knew Then What You Know Now." IHT Rendezvous, *International Herald Tribune*, May 10, 2013. http://rendezvous.blogs.nytimes.com/2013/05/10/ if-you-knew-then-what-you-know-now/?_r=0.

Berger, Kate. "Schools: Helping Expat Kids to Adapt." *Financial Times*, July 25, 2017. https://propertylistings.ft.com/ propertynews/united-kingdom/5132-schools-helping-expat-kids-to-adapt.html.

Berger, Kate. "Helping Your Child Settle Into Life Abroad: Overcoming the Challenges, and Making the Most of the Benefits of Raising Children Abroad." *HSBC Expat Explorer Survey 2016*, May 1, 2017. https://www.expatexplorer.hsbc.com/survey/ family/helping-children-settle-in.

Berger, Kate. "Helping Expat Children Adjust to Life Abroad." *Telegraph*, April 20, 2011. http://www.telegraph.co.uk/expat/expat-life/8459272/Helping-expat-children-adjust-to-life-abroad.html.

Berlitz Consulting. "Global Expatriates Observatory – White Paper 2011." *Berlitz Consulting*. http://www.berlitz.com/SiteData/ docs/WhitePaper/f476729acac735d4/White Paper Expatriation Survey 2011.pdf

Black, Stewart J. and Mark Mendenhall. "The U-Curve Adjustment Hypothesis Revisited: A Review and Theoretical Framework." *Journal of International Business Studies*, Vol. 22, No. 2 (2nd Qtr., 1991): 225-247. http://www.researchgate.net/profile/Mark_ Mendenhall/publication/5222549_The_U-Curve_Adjustment_ Hypothesis_Revisited_A_Review_and_Theoretical_Framework/ links/00b4952b85b17945a8000000.pdf.

Black, Stewart J. and Hal B. Gregersen, "The Other Half of the Picture: Antecedents of Spouse Cross-Cultural Adjustment," *Journal of International Business Studies,* Vol. 22, No. 3 (3rd Qtr., 1991): 461-477. http://www.researchgate.net/profile/Hb_Gre-gersen/publication/5222559_The_Other_Half_of_the_Pic-ture_Antecedents_of_Spouse_Cross-Cultural_Adjustment/ links/0f3175327065e37d0c000000.pdf.

Blanke, Jennifer and Thea Chiesa (eds.). "The Travel & Tourism Competitiveness Report 2013." World Economic Forum, 2013. http://www3.weforum.org/docs/WEF_TT_Competitiveness_Report_2013.pdf.

Bolden, McGill, Claire. "Expat Experiences Through the Decades: How the Internet has Changed the Expat Experience." *Global Living Magazine*, Issue 12, May/June 2014. mailto:http://globallivingmagazine.com/expat-experiences-through-the-decades/.

Bolon, Anne-Sophie. "Nowhere to Call Home But I Like Being a Global Nomad." *New York Times,* October 26, 2002. http://www.nytimes.com/2002/10/26/news/26iht-rkid_ed3_.html.

Brookfield Global Relocation Services. "2016 Global Mobility Trends." http://globalmobilitytrends.bgrs.com/.

Brookfield Global Relocation Services. "Mindful Mobility: 2015 Global Mobility Trends Survey Report." Link no longer available.

Brookfield Global Relocation Services. "2013 Global Relocation Trends Survey."

Brookfield Global Relocation Services. 2012 Global Relocation Trends Survey." Link no longer available.

Brown, Robert J. "Dominant Stressors on Expatriate Couples During International Assignments." *The International Journal of Human Resource Management*, Vol. 19, No. 6, (June 2008): 1018-1034.

Cadden, Michael and Andrew Kitell. "Shrinking World, Broadening Horizons – Changes in International Relocation in the 21st Century." Families in Global Transition (FIGT) Articles on International Relocation Trends in the 21st Century. http://www.figt.org/relocation_trends.

Cai, Deborah A. and José I. Rodriguez. "Adjusting to Cultural Differences: The Intercultural Adaptation Model." *Intercultural Communication Studies* Vol. 1, No. 2, 1996-7.

Caligiuri, Paula M. "Selecting Expatriates for Personality Characteristics: A Moderating Effect of Personality on the Relationship Between Host National Contact and Cross-Cultural Adjustment." Management International Review, Vol. 40, No. 1 (2001): 61-80. http://smtp.tmscenterofnj.com/sites/default/files/Selecting Expatriates for Personality Characteristics.pdf.

Caligiuri, Paula, Jean Phillips, Mila Lazarova, Ibraiz Tarique and Peter Bürgi. "The Theory of Met Expectations Applied to Expatriate Adjustment: The Role of Cross-cultural Training." The International Journal of Human Resource Management, Volume 12, Issue 3 (May 2001): 357-372.

Cartus. "2012 Trends in Global Relocation – Global Mobility Policy and Practices Survey." May 2012. Link no longer available.

Castro, Maria. "NYC as the Ultimate TCK City." Denizen Magazine, March 2009. http://www.denizenmag.com/2009/03/nyc-is-the-ultimate-tck-city/.

Citron, Jim and Vija Mendelson. "Coming Home: Relationships, Roots and Unpacking." Transitions Abroad Magazine, July/August 2005. http://www.transitionsabroad.com/publications/magazine/0507/coming_home_from_study_abroad.shtml.

Clegg, Alicia. "The Trials of Long-Distance Life." Financial Times, February 6, 2013. http://www.ft.com/intl/cms/s/0/886747f6-6a42-11e2-a7d2-00144feab49a.html - axzz2Q9WNFSvu.

Clegg, Alicia. "Tales From Trailing Husbands." Financial Times, June 10, 2013. https://www.ft.com/content/0227c0e0-cdf1-11e2-a13e-00144feab7de.

Cohen, Roger. "The Quest to Belong." New York Times, November 28, 2013. http://www.nytimes.com/2013/11/29/opinion/cohen-the-quest-to-belong.html.

"Coming Home – Resources from the Metro Boston Students Study Abroad Reentry Conference." October 15, 2005. http://www.calvin.edu/academic/off-campus/instructors/re-entry.pdf.

"Communication Across Cultures in Practice." Internations Magazine. http://www.internations.org/magazine/intercultural-communication-15409/communication-across-cultures-in-practice-3.

Coutu, Diane L. "How Resilience Works." Harvard Business Review, May 2002.

Cox, Pamela L, Raihan H. Khan and Kimberly A. Armani. "Repatriate Adjustment and Turnover: The Role of Expectations and Perceptions." *Review of Business and Finance Studies*, Vol. 4, No. 1 (2013). http://papers.ssrn.com/sol3/papers. cfm?abstract_id=2155176.

Crain, Caleb. "Subcontinental Drift." *New York Times*, July 11, 1999. http://www.nytimes.com/books/99/07/11/ reviews/990711.11craint.html.

Cullins, Rachael, "Three Personality Traits that Make a Successful Expat," October 6, 2011. https://whywaittoseetheworld.com/ personality-traits-successful-expat-2/.

"Cultural Awareness." *Internations Magazine*. http://www.internations.org/magazine/cultural-awareness-15426.

"Cultural Intelligence." *Internations Magazine*. http://www.internations.org/magazine/cultural-intelligence-15334.

Dedyukhina, Anastasia. "How Technology Killed the Work-Life Balance" *Consciously Digital*, May 31, 2017. http://www.consciously-digital.com/blog/ how-technology-killed-the-work-life-balance.

"Defining Culture." *Internations Magazine*. http://www.internations.org/magazine/intercultural-communication-15409/ defining-culture-2

Devi, Sharmila. "Commuters Going the Extra Mile." *Financial Times*, March 8, 2012. http://www.ft.com/intl/cms/s/0/85086dbe-4e51-11e1-aa0b-00144feabdc0.html - axzz2Q9WNFSvu.

Dickinson, Nancy. "Championing Dual Careers: Promoting Successful International Assignments." *Re-locate Magazine*, Autumn 2017.

Dizik, Alina. "Expat Life: Making it Work for Your Kids." *BBC Capital*, June 10, 2015. http://www.bbc.com/capital/ story/20150609-happy-kids-happy-expat-life.

Domnick, Heather. "When Pulling Your Hair Out Just Isn't Enough: 15 Ways to Cure the Stressed Out Expat." *Expat Exchange*. http://www.expatexchange.com/lib. cfm?networkID=159&articleID=2738.

Downes, Meredith, Iris I. Warner and Masoud Hemmasi. "Individual Profiles as Predictors of Expatriate Effectiveness." *Competitiveness Review*, Vol. 20, No.3 (2010): 235-247.

Ernst & Young. "Global Generations: A Global Study on Work-Life Challenges Across Generations." 2015. http://www.ey.com/Publication/vwLUAssets/EY-global-generations-a-global-study-on-work-life-challenges-across-generations/$FILE/EY-global-generations-a-global-study-on-work-life-challenges-across-generations.pdf.

Expat Communication. "Global Survey 2017: Impact of Expatriation on Couples and Dual Careers." June 26, 2017. http://www.expatcommunication.com/en/impact-of-expatriation-on-couples-and-dual-careers/.

Fagan, Chelsea. "What Happens When You Live Abroad." *Thought Catalog*, May 21, 2012. http://thoughtcatalog.com/2012/what-happens-when-you-live-abroad/.

"'Family Matters!' Report on the key findings of the ExpatExpert.com/AMJ Campbell International Relocation Survey", *ExpatExpert.com*, September 2008. http://www.expatexpert.com/pdf/Report_on_Key_Findings_of_Family_Matters_Survey.pdf.

Feiler, Bruce. "The Stories That Bind Us." *New York Times*, March 15, 2013. http://www.nytimes.com/2013/03/17/fashion/the-family-stories-that-bind-us-this-life.html?pagewanted=all.

Feintzeig, Rachel. "After Stints Abroad, Re-Entry Can Be Hard." *Wall Street Journal*, September 17, 2013. http://online.wsj.com/article/SB10001424127887323342404579081382781895274.html.

Finaccord. "Global Expatriates: Size, Segmentation and Forecast for the Worldwide Market." *Finaccord*, January 20, 2014. http://finaccord.com/uk/report_global-expatriates_size-segmentation-and-forecast-for-the-worldwide-market.htm.

Fisher, Max. "A Surprising Map of the Countries That Are Most And Least Welcoming to Foreigners." *Washington Post*, March 21, 2013. http://www.washingtonpost.com/blogs/worldviews/wp/2013/03/21/a-fascinating-map-of-countries-color-coded-by-their-openness-to-foreigners/

Fitzgerald, Nora. "For Teens, it's a Tough Transition." *New York Times,* June 26, 2004. http://www.nytimes. com/2004/06/26/news/26iht-rteen_ed3_.html

Foley, Maria. "Moving Back Home After Living Overseas." *I was an expat wife,* April 29, 2013. http://iwasanexpatwife. com/2013/04/29/moving-back-home-after-living-overseas/. (blog post no longer available, blog now marked as 'private'.)

Foley, Maria. "Battling re-entry shock." *I was an expat wife,* December 10, 2012. http://iwasanexpatwife.com/2012/12/10/ battling-re-entry-shock/. (blog post no longer available, blog now marked as 'private'.)

Foley, Maria. "What you need to know about the Big Five and expat adjustment." I was an expat wife, April 4, 2011. (blog post no longer available, blog now marked as 'private'.)

Fondas, Nanette. "The Many Myths About Mothers Who 'Opt Out.'" *The Atlantic,* March 25, 2013. http://www.theatlantic.com/sexes/archive/2013/03/ the-many-myths-about-mothers-who-opt-out/274354/.

"Four Common Stages of Cultural Adjustment." https://www.prince ton.edu/oip/practical-matters/Cultural-Adjustment.pdf.

Frost, Dana. "Repatriation: Tips and Advice to Ease the Transition." *Expat Women: Tips & Checklists,* September 2010. http://www. expatwomen.com/expat-women-tips-checklists/repatriation-tips- and-advice-to-ease-the-transition-dana-frost.php.

Garone, Elizabeth. "Expat Culture Shock Boomerangs in the Office." *BBC,* June 11, 2012. http://www.bbc.com/capital/ story/20130611-returning-expat-culture-shock.

Gidley, Apple. "Expatriates and Repatriates Experience Equal Doses of Culture Shock." *Telegraph,* December 29, 2010. http://www. telegraph.co.uk/expat/expatlife/8228026/Expatriates-and-repatri- ates-experience-equal-doses-of-culture-shock.html.

Gillme, Anne. "Expatriates: The Invisible Force Ruling Your Mar- riage (and All Your Relationships)." *Expatriate Connection.* http://expatriateconnection.com/expatriates-the-invisi- ble-force-ruling-your-marriage-and-all-your-relationships/.

Giridharadas, Anand. "The Struggle of The Global Placeless." *New York Times*, March 26, 2010. http://www.nytimes. com/2010/03/27/us/27iht-currents.html?_r=0.

Glassie, John. "The Way We Live Now: Questions for Jhumpa Lahiri." *New York Times*, September 7, 2003. http://www.nytimes. com/2003/09/07/magazine/the-way-we-live-now-9-7-03-questions-for-jhumpa-lahiri-crossing-over.html.

Graebel International and The Interchange Institute. "Moving Matters: A Study of How to Help International Transferees Relocate." Final Report, Fall 2005. http://www.interchangeinstitute.org/files/GraebelMovingMattersFinalReportMarch2006.pdf

Greenfield, Beth. "The World's Friendliest Countries." *Forbes*, October 24, 2012. http://www.forbes.com/sites/ bethgreenfield/2012/10/24/the-worlds-friendliest-countries-3/

Greenfield, Beth. "The World's Friendliest Countries." *Forbes*, January 6, 2012. http://www.forbes.com/sites/ bethgreenfield/2012/01/06/the-worlds-friendliest-countries-2/

Greenfield, Beth, "The World's Friendliest Countries," *Forbes*, April 8, 2011. http://www.forbes.com/2011/04/08/worlds-friendliest-countries-business-expats.html.

Hallet Mobbs, Carole. "Can Our Worldview be 'Multiple?'" *Your Expat Child*, April 15, 2013. http://expatchild.com/ can-our-worldview-be-multiple/?utm_source=feedburner&utm_medium=email&utm_campaign=Feed%3A+YourExpatChild+%28Your+Expat+Child%29.

Hart, Alexa. "7 Ways to Meet People and Build a Community of Friends Abroad." *Feedbacq Blog*, http://www.feedbacq.com/blog/7-ways-to-meet-people-and-build-a-community-of-friends-abroad/.

Hatfield, Madeleine. "Repatriates and the Value of Intercultural Skills." *Nothing to write home about*, March 17, 2013. http://madeleinehatfield.com/2013/03/17/ repatriates-and-the-value-of-intercultural-skills/.

Hatfield, Madeleine. "Repatriation and the Reality of Going Home." *Your Expat Child*, May 3, 2013. http://expatchild.com/ repatriation-reality-going-home/.

Heyden, Tom. "The Adults Who Suffer Extreme Homesickness." *BBC News Magazine,* June 5, 2013. http://www.bbc.co.uk/news/magazine-22764986.

Howe-Walsh, Liza. "Repatriation: Furthering the Research Agenda through the Lens of Commitment, Uncertainty Reduction and Social Cognitive Career Theories." *International Journal of Business and Management,* Vol. 8, No. 16 (July 16, 2013). http://dx.doi.org/10.5539/ijbm.v8n16p1.

HSBC. "Expat Explorer Surveys 2010, 2011 and 2012." http://www.expatexplorer.hsbc.com/ - /pages/about.

HSBC. "Expat Explorer: Achieving Ambitions Abroad." *HSBC Global Report,* 2016. https://www.expatexplorer.hsbc.com/survey/files/pdfs/overall-reports/2016/HSBC_Expat_Explorer_2016_report.pdf.

Hu, Elise. "Facebook Makes Us Sadder And Less Satisfied, Study Finds." *NPR,* Augusts 20, 2013. http://www.npr.org/blogs/alltechconsidered/2013/08/19/213568763/researchers-facebook-makes-us-sadder-and-less-satisfied.

Humphrey, Louise. "Finding a Family Support Network." *Mothering Matters,* April 1, 2016. https://motheringmatters.ch/0416fs/.

Hydrogen. "Global Professionals on the Move." Survey, Fifth Edition, 2014. "Summary of the report available at https://www.slideshare.net/Hydrogen_Group/global-professionals-on-the-move-2014.

"Identities." *NPR Ted Radio Hour,* May 8, 2015. http://www.npr.org/2013/10/06/229879937/identities.

The Interchange Institute. "Many Women, Many Voices: A Study of Accompanying Spouses Around the World." Prudential Financial, 2005. http://www.interchangeinstitute.org/files/MWMVFinal05.pdf.

Internations. "Expat Insider 2015." https://www.internations.org/expat-insider/2015/.

"I Have Moved 82 times." Interview with Andrew Berglund, as told to Song Jung-a, *Financial Times,* January 31/February 1, 2009. Link no longer available.

"Intercultural Competence." *Internations Magazine.* http://www. internations.org/magazine/intercultural-competence-15422.

International Organization for Migration (IOM). "World Migration Report 2010." http://www.publications.iom.int.

Jalongo, Mary Renck. "Helping Children to Cope With Relocation." *Childhood Education,* Vol. 71, No. 2 (Winter 1994). http://www. freepatentsonline.com/article/Childhood-Education/16551206.html.

Javidan, Mansour. "What is Global Mindset?" Presentation, Global Mindset Institute, March 2011. https://www.mgsm.mq.edu. au/assets/PDF/Other-PDF-Files/Global-Mindset-Javidan-March-2011.pdf.

Javidan, Mansour. "Global Mindset Defined: Expat Success Strategy." Research by the Worldwide ERC Foundation for Workforce Mobility and Thunderbird School of Global Management. Preview of the research available at https://www.scribd.com/document/62070349/Global-Mindset-Defined.

Javidan, Mansour. Mary Teagarden and David Bowen. "Global Mindset Secrets of Superstar Expats." *Knowledge Network,* Thunderbird School of Global Management, December 20, 2012. https://thunderbird.asu.edu/knowledge-network/secrets-superstar-expats.

Jones, Jerry. "The Seven Lies of Living Cross-Culturally." *The Culture Blend,* April 10, 2015. http://www.thecultureblend. com/the-seven-lies-of-living-cross-culturally/.

Katona, Peter. "More and More Americans Consider Themselves 'Hidden Immigrants.'" *Columbia University News Service,* February 27, 2007. http://jscms.jrn.columbia.edu/cns/2007-02-27/katona-thirdculturekids.html.

Katz, Stephanie. "The 'Trailing Spouse' no Longer Need Be Such a Drag." *Expat Arrivals.* http://www.expatarrivals.com/article/the-trailing-spouse-no-longer-need-be-such-a-drag.

Kite, Hanna. "Rooted to Nowhere." *Time,* October 20, 2003. http:// www.time.com/time/magazine/article/0,9171,524622,00.html.

Koblow, Sarah. "Resilience: Learning How to Fly Like Eagles." in Parfitt, Jo (ed.), *Forced to Fly,* 2nd ed., Summertime Publishing, 2012.

Konnikova, Maria. "How People Learn to Become Resilient."
*New Yorker*, February 11, 2016. http://www.newyorker.com/
science/maria-konnikova/the-secret-formula-for-resilience

Konnikova, Maria. "How Facebook Makes Us Unhappy." *New Yorker*,
September 10, 2013. http://www.newyorker.com/tech/elements/
how-facebook-makes-us-unhappy

KPMG. "Global Assignment Policies and Practices." Survey 2015.
https://www.kpmg.com/Global/en/IssuesAndInsights/Articles-
Publications/Documents/global-assignment-policies-and-prac-
tices-survey-2015-v2.pdf.

Kristal, Jill. "Community Spirit Kills Homesickness." *Telegraph*,
October 13, 2003. http://www.telegraph.co.uk/expat/4190284/
Community-spirit-kills-homesickness.html

Kuper, Simon. "Moving Experiences." *Financial Times*,
January 30, 2009. http://www.ft.com/intl/cms/s/0/fc3a83f4-ed9c-
11dd-bd60-0000779fd2ac.html - axzz2Q9WNFSvu.

LaBrack, Bruce. "Ten Top Immediate Re-entry Challenges." http://
ww2.odu.edu/ao/oip/studyabroad/resources/toptenreentry.pdf.

LaBrack, Bruce. "Preparing to Return Home: Quick Tips." http://ww2.
odu.edu/ao/oip/studyabroad/resources/preparingtoreturn.pdf.

LaBrack, Bruce. "Theory Reflections: Cultural Adaptations, Culture
Shock and the 'Curves of Adjustment'." http://www.nafsa.org/_/
file/_/theory_connections_adjustment.pdf.

Laing, Olivia. "The Future of Loneliness." *The Guardian*,
April 1, 2015. http://www.theguardian.com/society/2015/apr/01/
future-of-loneliness-internet-isolation.

Lang, Gretchen. "Often More Accomplished, But Sometimes More
Troubled." *New York Times*, October 26, 2002. http://www.
nytimes.com/2002/10/26/news/26iht-rreturn_ed3_.html.

Le Chevalier, Gisèle. "Teaching Sophie Her Cultural Heritage."
*Denizen Magazine*, July 2011. http://www.denizenmag.
com/2011/07/showing-sophie-her-cultural-heritage/.

Little, Brian. "Who Are You, Really? The Puzzle of Personality." *TED Talk*. https://www.ted.com/talks/
brian_little_who_are_you_really_the_puzzle_of_personality

Livermore, David. "Sit Still and Improve Your CQ: The Power of Reflection." https://culturalq.com/ sit-still-and-improve-your-cq-the-power-of-reflection/.

Lublin, Joann S. "Married Executives Juggle International Moves." *Wall Street Journal,* September 19, 2010. http://online.wsj.com/article/ SB10001424052748703440604575496091462406002.html.

Mahoney, Sheelagh and Gustavo Aranda. "Can You Afford to Throw Away £2 Million of Your Organisation's Money on a Failed Expat Assignment?" *Business Reporter,* May 25, 2015. http://business-reporter.co.uk/2015/05/21/can-you-afford-to-throw-away-2-million-of-your-organisations-money-on-a-failed-expat-assignment/.

Marche, Stephen, "Is Facebook Making Us Lonely?," *The Atlantic,* April 2, 2012. http://www.theatlantic.com/magazine/ archive/2012/05/is-facebook-making-us-lonely/308930/

Marks, Dougie. "Combating the Stress of Moving Abroad." *The Guardian,* July 17, 2008. https://www.theguardian.com/ money/2008/jul/17/expat-finance-health.

Marston, Rebecca. "Exodus: Movement of Rich People – a Life at Home Abroad." *BBC News* – Business, December 5, 2011. http:// www.bbc.co.uk/news/business-15696714.

Matt, Susan J. "The New Globalist is Homesick." *New York Times,* March 21, 2012. http://www.nytimes.com/2012/03/22/opinion/ many-still-live-with-homesickness.html?pagewanted=all.

McCaig, Norma. "Growing Up With a World View: Nomad Children Develop Multicultural Skills." *Foreign Service Journal* (September 1994): 32-41.

Merchant, Nilofer. "Feel Like You Don't Fit in? Here's How to Find Where You Truly Belong." *IDEAS.TED.COM,* August 30, 2017. https://ideas.ted.com/feel-like-you-dont-fit-in-heres-how-to-find-where-you-truly-belong/.

Minton-Eversole, Theresa. "Best Expatriate Assignments Require Much Thought, Even More Planning." *HR Magazine,* December 2008. http://findarticles.com/p/articles/mi_m3495/ is_12_53/ai_n31169733.

Monahan, Patrick. "Supportive Relationships Linked to Willingness to Pursue Opportunities." *Carnegie Mellon University*, Dietrich College of Humanities and Social Sciences, 2017. https://www.cmu.edu/dietrich/news/news-stories/2017/august/supportive-spouses-brooke-feeny.html.

"More People Than Ever Are Living Abroad." *Associated Press*, September 11, 2013. https://www.independent.ie/world-news/more-people-than-ever-living-abroad-29573055.html.

"Moving Overseas With Children: Preparing Your Child." *Expat Info Desk*, October 17, 2011. http://www.expat-infodesk.com/expat-guide/moving-with-your-children/dealing-with-different-ages/.

"Moving with kids." *InterNations Blog*, August 2011. http://blog.internations.org/2011/08/5088/.

Nayar, Vineet. "The Power of Intention." *Harvard Business Review*, February 18, 2013. https://hbr.org/2013/02/the-power-of-intent.

"New Research Reveals the Difficulties Faced by Expats." *Relocate Magazine*, April 26, 2017. https://www.relocatemagazine.com/articles/health-new-research-reveals-the-difficulties-faced-by-cxpats-.

Oberg, Kalervo. "Cultural Shock: Adjustment to New Cultural Environments." (reprint) *Practical Anthropology*, 1960, Vol. 7: 177-182. http://agem-cthnomedizin.de/download/cu29_2-3_2006_S_142-146_Repr_Oberg.pdf.

O'Connell Anne. "How to Make a Transition Abroad Easier on the Kids." *The Wall Street Journal*, June 18, 2015. https://blogs.wsj.com/expat/2015/06/18/how-to-make-a-transition-abroad-easier-on-the-kids/.

Oesterreich, Lesia. "Understanding Children: Moving to a New Home." Pamphlet, Iowa State University. University Extension, 2004. http://www.extension.iastate.edu/Publications/PM1529G.pdf.

Oishi, Shigehiro and Ulrich Shimmack. "Residential Mobility, Well-Being and Mortality." *Journal of Personality and Social Psychology*, Vol. 98, No. 6 (2010): 980-994. http://www.midus.wisc.edu/findings/pdfs/831.pdf.

Onley, Dawn S. "Avert Assignment Failure: Support Spouses in Overseas Relocations." *Society for Human Resource Management*, March 13, 2014. https://www.shrm.org/ResourcesAndTools/hr-topics/global-hr/Pages/Spouses-Overseas-Relocations.aspx.

Owens, Susan. "Expat Lives: A Sense for Style." *Financial Times*, June 22, 2012. http://www.ft.com/intl/cms/s/2/cf7aaee8-b60c-11e1-a511-00144feabdc0.html.

Paul, Pamela. "Does Moving a Child Create Adult Baggage?" *New York Times*, July 9, 2010.

Permits Foundation. "International Mobility and Dual Career Survey of International Employers." The Hague: Permits Foundation, July 2012. Last accessed 30 November 2017. https://www.permitsfoundation.com/wp-content/uploads/2013/04/Permits-Global-Employers-Survey-2012.pdf.

Permits Foundation. "Expatriate Spouses and Partners Employment, Work Permits and International Mobility – International Survey Summary Report." December 2008. https://www.permitsfoundation.com/wp-content/uploads/2013/04/Spousal-survey-new-style.pdf.

Petriglieri, Gianpiero. "Moving Around Without Losing Your Roots." *Harvard Business Review Blog Network*, October 2012. http://blogs.hbr.org/cs/2012/10/moving_around_without_losing_your_roots.html.

PricewaterhouseCoopers. "International Assignments: Global Policy and Practice Key Trends 2005." *PricewaterhouseCoopers*, p.28.

PricewaterhouseCoopers. "Talent Mobility 2020: The Next Generation of International Assignments." *PricewaterhouseCoopers*, 2010. http://www.pwc.com/gx/en/managing-tomorrows-people/future-of-work/pdf/talent-mobility-2020.pdf.

PricewaterhouseCoopers. "Talent Mobility 2020 and Beyond." *PricewaterhouseCoopers*, 2012. https://press.pwc.com/Multimedia/image/Talent-mobility-2020-and-beyond/a/f81b0788-4b81-4fe2-a6d1-b6d279352b32.

Ramsey, Nancy. "Social Networking: A Cure for Reverse Culture Shock?" *ABC News*, July 22, 2010. Link no longer available.

Ramsey, Sheila J. "Living Through Change,. *Transition Dynamics*, March 2001. http://www.transition-dynamics.com/ltchange.html.

Ramsey, Sheila J. and Barbara Schaetti. "Reentry: Coming 'Home' to the Unfamiliar." *Transition Dynamics*, November 1999. http://www.transition-dynamics.com/reentry.html.

Reiche, Sebastian. "The Key to Successful Expatriation Lies More in Developing Appropriate Skills Than in Possessing Favorable Personality Traits? Some Evidence," *Expatriatus*, IESE Business School, University of Navarra (Spain), September 7, 2012. http://blog.iese.edu/expatriatus/2012/09/07/the-key-to-successful-expatriation-lies-more-in-developing-appropriate-skills-than-in-possessing-favorable-personality-traits-some-evidence/.

Reiche, Sebastian. "Expatriate Adjustment: Is There Always a 'Honeymoon?'" *Expatriatus*, IESE Business School, University of Navarra (Spain), October 28, 2011. http://blog.iese.edu/expatriatus/2011/10/28/expatriate-adjustment-is-there-always-a-'honeymoon'/.

Reiche, Sebastian. "Social Media Help to Ease 'Expat Blues." *Expatriatus*, IESE Business School, University of Navarra (Spain), June 9, 2011. http://blog.iese.edu/expatriatus/2011/06/09/social-media-help-to-ease-"expat-blues"/.

"Research Your Relocation: What Resources Make the Most Successful Move?" from Expat Women: Tips & Checklists. http://www.expatwomen.com/expat-women-tips-checklists/research-relocation-what-resources-help-make-most-successful-move.php.

Roberts, Elizabeth. "Expat Problems: How to Cope with the Biggest Ones." *Telegraph*, September 2, 2015.

Roese, Neal J. "Being Too Busy for Friends Won't Help Your Career." *Harvard Business Review*, July 28, 2017. https://hbr.org/2017/07/being-too-busy-for-friends-wont-help-your-career.

Schaetti, Barbara. "Families on the Move; Working Together to Meet the Challenge." *Transition Dynamics*. http://www.transition-dynamics.com/fotm.html.

Schaetti, Barbara F. and Carol Grose, "Mover and Shaker," *FOCUS News*, Vol. 50, No. 1 (December 2001/January 2002): 10-11. http://www.transition-dynamics.com/movershaker.html.

Schaetti, Barbara F. and Sheila J. Ramsey. "The Expatriate Family: Practicing Practical Leadership." *Mobility*, Employee Relocation Council, May 1999. http://www.transition-dynamics.com/expat-family.html.

Schmidt, Patrick. "Ursula Brinkmann: An Interview With One of the Leading Specialists in Intercultural Interventions." *SIETAR Europa Journal* (June-August 2014).

Schuler, Corinna. "When No Place Feels Like Home." *The Christian Science Monitor*, December 23, 2003. http://www.csmonitor.com/2003/1223/p14s02-legn.html.

Shaffer, M. A., Harrison, D. A., Gregersen, H. B., Black, J. S. and Ferzandi, L. A. "You Can Take It With You: Individual Differences And Expatriate Effectiveness." *Journal of Applied Psychology*, Vol. 91, No. 1 (2006): 109-125.

Shakya, Holly B. et. al. "Association of Facebook Use With Compromised Well-Being: A Longitudinal Study," *American Journal of Epidemiology*, Vol. 185, Iss. 3 (1 February 2017): 203–211. https://academic.oup.com/aje/article-abstract/185/3/203/2915143?redirectedFrom=fulltext.

Shortland, Sue. "Family Support: Policy Implications for Domestic and International Moves." *Re-locate Magazine*, Autumn 2017.

Society for Human Resource Management. "Managing International Assignments." May 1, 2017. https://www.shrm.org/resourcesand-tools/tools-and-samples/toolkits/pages/cms_010358.aspx.

"The Attraction of Solitude." *Economist*, August 25, 2012. http://www.economist.com/node/21560844?fsrc=scn/fb/wl/pe/attractionofsolitude.

"The Dark Side of the Expat Life." *International Herald Tribune*, March 21, 2013. http://rendezvous.blogs.nytimes.com/2013/03/21/the-dark-side-of-the-expat-life/.

TheMIGroup. "The Trailing Male Spouse." *Relocate Magazine*, October 19, 2016. https://www.relocatemagazine.com/articles/mobility-industry-the-trailing-male-spouse.

Twentyman, Jessica. "An Expat Job Can Be a Move Too Far." *Financial Times*, October 7, 2010. http://www.ft.com/intl/cms/s/0/c1d1b668-d22b-11df-8fbe-00144feabdc0.html.

"Up or Out: Next Moves for the Modern Expatriate." Economist Intelligence Unit, 2010. http://graphics.eiu.com/upload/eb/LON_PL_Regus_WEB2.pdf.

U.S. Census Bureau. "Profile America Facts For Features: Unmarried and Single Americans Week: September 17-23, 2017," August 16, 2017. https://www.census.gov/newsroom/facts-for-features/2017/single-americans-week.html .

Valcour, Monique. "The Dual-Career Mojo that Makes Couples Thrive." blog post, *Harvard Business Review Blog Network*, April 11, 2013. https://hbr.org/2013/04/the-dual-career-mojo-that-make.

Van Bochaute, Ellen. "What Expatriate Children Never Tell Their Parents." http://www2.leuvion.com/wp-content/uploads/2018/01/Expat-Kids.pdf.

Vannucci, Anna et. al. "Social Media Use and Anxiety in Emerging Adults." *Journal of Affective Disorders*, Vol. 207, (January 1 2017): 163-166. http://www.jad-journal.com/article/S0165-0327(16)30944-2/fulltext.

Volpi, David. "Heavy Technology Use Linked to Fatigue, Stress and Depression in Young Adults." *Huffington Post,* October 2, 2012. https://www.huffingtonpost.com/david-volpi-md-pc-facs/technology-depression_b_1723625.html.

Ward, Russel. "The Expat, the Writer, the Worker." *In Search of a Life Less Ordinary,* March 1, 2013. https://insearchofalifelessordinary.com/2013/03/the-expat-writer-worker/.

Warwick-Ching, Lucy. "Ten Worst Mistakes Made by Expats." *Financial Times,* August 11, 2011. http://www.ft.com/intl/cms/s/0/f75bc8d8-c3f6-11e0-b302-00144feabdc0.html - axzz2Q9WNFSvu.

Whyte, David. "The House of Belonging." 1996.

Wilcox, Quenby. "Dual-Career Challenges for the Expat Family: Why Expat Employers Should Be Concerned." *Huffington Post,* December 11, 2013. http://www.huffingtonpost.com/quenby-wilcox-/dualcareer-challenges-for-the-expat-family_b_4421109.html.

Wilson, Wendy and Claire Snowdon. "The Future of Modern Mobility." *International HR Adviser*, Winter 2012. http://www.internationalhradviser.com/storage/downloads/The%20Future%20Of%20Modern%20Mobility.pdf.

Winkelman, Michael. "Cultural Shock and Adaptation." *Journal of Counseling and Development*, Vol. 73, Iss. 2 (November-December 1994): 121-126. https://www.researchgate.net/publication/232455059_Cultural_Shock_and_Adaptation.

Wittenberg-Cox, Aviva. "If You Can't Find a Spouse Who Supports Your Career, Stay Single." *Harvard Business Review*, 24 October 2017. https://hbr.org/2017/10/if-you-cant-find-a-spouse-who-supports-your-career-stay-single.

World Economic Forum. "Stimulating Economies Through Fostering Talent Mobility." 2010. http://www.weforum.org/pdf/ip/ps/TalentMobility.pdf.

"World Expat Population – The Numbers." *Feedbacq Blog*. http://www.feedbacq.com/blog/world-expat-population-the-numbers/.

Wu, Zhu. "The Lived Experience of Being a Foreigner." *Phenomenology Online*. http://www.phenomenologyonline.com/sources/textorium/wu-zhou-the-lived-experience-of-being-a-foreigner/.

Yates, Rachel. "Relocation Policies: Are We Being Set Up to Fail?" *Expat Women Blog*, March 20, 2012. http://expatwomen.blogspot.ch/2012/03/relocation-policies-are-we-being-set-up.html.

Yates, Rachel. "How to Survive Moving Your Kids to a New School, District, City, State or Country…Four Basic Rules for Transitioning Children." *FIGT Blog*, June 16, 2013. http://www.figt.org/blog/1319755.

Yeaton, Kathryn and Nicole Hall. "Expatriates: Reducing Failure Rates." *The Journal of Corporate Accounting and Finance*, Wiley Periodicals Inc., (March/April 2008): 75-78.

Young, Rudolph. "Is There a Perfect Personality for Expatriates?" *Chronicle of Higher Education*, April 3, 2011a. http://chronicle.com/article/Is-There-a-Perfect-Personality/126964/.

Young, Rudolph. "Cross-Cultural Skills: Essential for Expatriate Success." *Chronicle of Higher Education*, August 23, 2011b. http://chronicle.com/article/Cross-Cultural-Skills-/128782/.

Young, Rudolph. "For Academic Expatriates, Families Can Be a Big Risk Factor." *Chronicle of Higher Education*, September 28, 2011c. http://www.chronicle.com/article/For-Academic-Expatriates/129151.

Zavrski-Makaric, Dina. "Building an Expat Identity: Who am I if I'm not from here?" http://www.expatexchange.com/settlingin.cfm?week=16&type=post.

"6 Personality Traits of a Happy Expat." *Expat Info Desk Blog*, November 16, 2010. http://www.expatinfodesk.com/blog/2010/11/16/6-personality-traits-of-a-happy-expat/.

# ABOUT THE AUTHOR

Katia Vlachos is a writer, coach and experienced expat. She writes on cross-cultural adaptation and the rewards and challenges of expatriate life. As a coach, she helps her clients navigate transitions, whether it is making an international move, changing career direction or coping with separation or divorce. Katia is a researcher and defense analyst by training, with a Ph.D. in Policy Analysis from the RAND Corporation and a masters in Public Policy from Harvard's Kennedy School of Government. She lives in Zurich, Switzerland.

She can be reached through her website as well as on social networks.

**www.katiavlachos.com**

Facebook: **@KatiaVlachosCoach**
Twitter: **@vlachosk**
LinkedIn: **Katia Vlachos**

**LID**
**ANNIVERSARY**

Sharing knowledge since 1993

- 1993 Madrid
- 2008 Mexico DF and Monterrey
- 2010 London
- 2011 New York and Buenos Aires
- 2012 Bogotá
- 2014 Shanghai